DISCOVERING
VINTAGE
Miami

DISCOVERING
VINTAGE
Miami

A Guide to the City's Timeless Shops,
Hotels, Restaurants & More

First Edition

MANDY BACA

Guilford, Connecticut
Helena, Montana
An imprint of Rowman & Littlefield

All the information in this guidebook is subject to change. We recommend that you call ahead to obtain current information before traveling.

Globe Pequot is an imprint of Rowman & Littlefield
Distributed by NATIONAL BOOK NETWORK

British Library Cataloguing in Publication information available

Library of Congress Cataloging-in-Publication data is available on file.

ISBN 978-1-4930-0745-5

∞™ The paper used in this publication meets the minimum requirements of American National Standard for Information Sciences—Permanence of Paper for Printed Library Materials, ANSI/NISO Z39.48-1992.

To all in Miami who keep history alive

Contents

About the Author

As a food- and history-obsessed Miami native, Mandy Baca found her true passion for food and writing while enrolled in the Hospitality School at Johnson & Wales University. She also holds a master's degree in Italian Gastronomy and Tourism from the University of Gastronomic Sciences in Colorno, Italy. She has contributed to various publications both locally and nationally and is the author of *The Sizzling History of Miami Cuisine: Cortaditos, Stone Crabs and Empanadas*, which details Miami's rich food culture. Mandy currently resides in Miami and continues her quest to inspire and advance the interest in local food culture.

Acknowledgments

I feel so grateful for the opportunity to write another book, which I hope will be an important historical reference for decades to come. I wanted to thank all those who made it possible.

First, I wanted to single out two specific individuals. Thank you to local writer Sara Liss, who forwarded this opportunity to me. Without her recommendation, this would have never come to fruition. Also, thank you to Tracee Williams, my editor at Globe Pequot, who was extremely patient with me. She was always on hand to assist me with any questions I had along the way.

Thanks to all the Miami locals who provided fantastic feedback, anecdotes, quotes, and general interest stories about their personal experiences not only at the establishments, but also of Miami and their own lives. In no particular order: Sef Gonzalez, Daniel Serfer, Lauren "Lolo" Reskin, Liz Tracy, Nathaniel Sandler, Ines Hegedus-Garcia, Cari Garcia, Malik Benjamin, Amy Rosenberg, Steve Roitstein, Washington Delgado, Carlos Olaechea, Aubrey Swanson, Marvin Tapia, Patricia Guarch Wise, Diego Ganoza, Zachary Fagenson, Matt Meltzer, and my dad, Jose Baca.

Finally, a huge and special thank you to all the owners, managers, and employees who welcomed me into their establishments, treated me like family, and provided me with great historical context and more personal experiences and stories that made each and every chapter that much more dynamic. In no particular order: Jorge Perez, Andrew Lister, Bob Penna, Theresa Ore, Marione Van Steensburg, Ota Zambrano, Mercy Gonzalez, Sandy Cobas, Ricardo Gutierrez, Renee Pasquarella, Tony Alarcon, Jorge Torres, Brian Alonso, Cheryl Mainzer, Vivian Jordan, Mary Holle, Eli Tako, Mike Bittel, Cecilia Curuthers, Fernando Montealegre, Jessica Bishop, Patrick Gleber, Kevin Rusk, Evan Chern, and David Laurenzo. I hope your establishments are open for decades to come for many more people to enjoy and create memories of their own.

Introduction

𝓘 like to play the game of Remember When . . . Older folks may remember the good ole days of Miami, when it was still a swamp town and the roads ended on 137th Avenue. Jai-alai was still popular, and Royal Castles were on every corner. When Jungle Island was Parrot Jungle and located in Pinecrest. What about the Serpentarium? Do you remember when Dadeland Mall first opened and when Mall of the Americas was actually Midway Mall? I can name countless restaurants that have met their demise due to time: Red Diamond

Italian, Pizza Palace, Wolfie's, and Rascal House. The historic Mary Elizabeth Hotel in Brownsville hung on until the early eighties. Krome Avenue was once no-man's-land and Bayfront Park housed a library. Holsum Bakery became the Bakery Center and finally Sunset Place. Don Carter's Bowling was once the hot spot.

Those are just some of Miami's long gone, but not forgotten, memories. And while I am a bit young to have lived most of Miami's best memories, I greatly enjoy the stories. I guess you could say that I am the last of a dying breed. It is fun to recount the old stories, the ones that remind us where we have been and where we are going.

In Miami, vintage is not only a state of time, but also a place. Vintage refers to the days of yesteryear in the old country. In the pages ahead you will find examples of such a concept. Some establishments may not have been around for more than twenty years, but their ambience takes you back to another country, another atmosphere, another soul.

Miami is a growing city in constant flux. In the short time I compiled establishments to include in this nostalgic book, four closed down. Let us observe a moment of silence for Van Dyke Cafe, Jimbo's, and Libreria Universal. And most fresh in the hearts of Miamians is the closing of Jumbo's Restaurant [1955–2014], best known for being the first restaurant in the city to integrate in the sixties and serving a mean fried shrimp. While the fates of Tobacco Road and Churchill's Pub hang in the balance, they are included in the book. Miami, a city known for killing its past, has closed down a variety of places with rich history and importance. Some of the few but not forgotten that went to the grave and are still talked about today like the Cubans at las ventanitas talk of the Cuba of yore include Wolfie's, Seven Seas, and The Embers. Whether you are a native or a tourist, it is not hard to see the history around you, with the Art Deco hotels along Ocean Drive and the old town of Coconut Grove, or even wonder how we got here.

In contrast to what many believe, the city of Miami and the greater South Florida region is not a historical wasteland. Our roots go back approximately 12,000 years with the first sightings of the Tequesta Indians near Deering Estate. A more populated and urbanized modern society would not develop in the area until the early 1800s.

While there are famous establishments with history that everyone knows, like Joe's Stone Crab and Tobacco Road, which are

highlighted in the pages ahead, I also wanted to feature the underdogs, the less widely known or celebrated in the media, but cherished by the local communities that support them. And while they may not be as historic as Tobacco Road, they are important as a symbol of history in our community. My hope is the same as many's: to support the local community, the people who run Miami and make it thrive, the good ole people working day in and day out for their passion and to transmit that passion to others. For those who are not so much into history, my hope is that they will visit the establishments noted in the book and also seek out their own adventures and historic spots, as well as continue the efforts to protect our historic places and spaces before they are taken over by big establishments trying to bland out our vibrant city. Visit these places because they may not be around for much longer and they are simply great establishments.

About 90 percent of the owners that I interviewed sang the same tune: You have to be passionate about what you do, and that is the only way you will survive. On the other side of the coin, the establishments' regular customers offer a different perspective reflecting the busy lifestyle of our consumerist society. You will not hear much on the news about the growth of a dry cleaner's down the street or a boutique hiring associates to sell children's clothing, but these are great success stories, too.

It is funny, when I first set out to do this project, I received a bit of pushback, especially from the owners or managers of the establishments. I think other writers reading this will understand. The big companies, the newer companies, have marketing plans in place or public relations pros to handle inquiries. Historically, people are naturally wary of writers. Or they do not feel that their place is of value to be written about. It is an interesting problem, as I see it. The new places vie for attention, for their time in the limelight, and the older places, well, they continue running their businesses the way they have done for decades. In their eyes, they do not need the press.

Like I always say, it is an odd place to call home and an odd place to have grown up, but I would not change it for any other experience. As you will note in the pages ahead, the exotic and foreign is commonplace, but I also portray establishments and peoples that are a bit off the beaten path. Miami is unlike any other part of the country, a place where different cultures, people, and mind-sets collide to make it one of a kind.

A&M COMICS

6650 BIRD RD. • MIAMI, FL 33155

(305) 661-3406

Preserving an American Art Form

Comic books emerged in 1933 as an outgrowth of comic strips. Like the Stephen Colberts and Jon Stewarts of our time, comic books served as comedic respite from the political churnings of the country. Initially a counterculture trend, anti-comic campaigns sprang up immediately, stating that they were unconstitutional and violent.

In 1949, decades before A&M Comics opened, an ordinance banning crime comic books passed in Miami. At large events throughout the city, children were forced to let go of their horror- and violence-packed comics; it was a scene straight out of the pages of the cult classic *Nineteen Eighty-Four*. An article in the October 5, 1949, *Miami News* included details of the now-absurd regulation: "The ordinance provides a $500 fine and/or 60 days in jail for any person who prints or sells any book, pamphlet, magazine, paper, etc., devoted to publication and principally made up of criminal news, police reports or accounts of criminal deed or pieces of stories of bloodshed, lust or crime." The ordinance was finally revoked in the late seventies, but it was not all roses thereafter.

The introduction of television in the fifties further impacted the popularity of comic books. In the eighties, big business became the largest providers of comic book products, making it difficult for the small stores to compete with the likes of Walmart and Toys "R" Us. A big factor that separates the small stores from the big retailers is that they carry rare items. While more mainstream than in prior decades, the comic book world remains in a state of flux, heavily

influenced by outside factors like the economy and the government—a trend that A&M Comics' owner, Jorge Perez, says will continue.

With over 200,000 comic books, 2,000 toys, and hundreds of graphic novels, A&M Comics is Miami's longest-running comic book store as well as one of the oldest in the country. Established in 1974 by a groovy couple from New York, Arnold and Maxine used their initials for the naming of the store, hence the moniker A&M. It occupied two other spaces in Miami before settling into its current location on the infamous Bird Road in 1974. Unlike the modern stores of today, A&M Comics stands as a nostalgic reminder of stores in the New York basement style—tiny, crammed, odd, and incense scented—amidst the uniform suburbia where it resides.

The store's exterior offers vintage signage and a poster-and-comic-book-plastered front window; once inside, every nook and cranny is strategically used, and while there is little organization to the items, the owner makes up for it in expertise and assistance. Prices are reasonable, ranging from $3 to $30 and upwards of hundreds of dollars for the more rare items. Among the coolest items in stock are early editions of Marvel Comics, previously known as Timely Comics. The store is so iconic that Joe Quesada, CCO of Marvel Comics, a comic book writer himself, came to the store for his first book signing.

Like A&M's original owners, Jorge Perez is also from New York. "My family came to Miami for the weather because of my asthma," he says. "In those days, Miami's climate was highly touted for its medicinal powers. We lived on Flagler Street, and we were the second Cuban family to live in our neighborhood. Those were different times; now the opposite is true. From a young age, I read Archie Comics, and a funny accident in junior high school sealed my fate. I lent a friend a dollar for his school lunch. Later that week, he did not have money to pay me back and instead paid me in five X-Men comic books. I have been a collector since that day, and before I became the owner of A&M Comics, I was a loyal customer of the store."

"As a key player in Miami's history," Jorge continues, "we try to be involved in the community as much as we can." Free Comic Book Day is equivalent to Record Store Day, a day for comic book stores and the community to come together. The spirited day is especially great for newbies interested in learning more about the world of comic books. Customers are allowed at least one free copy of a comic book from a selection of at least sixty different titles. Past titles have included Hello Kitty, *Guardians of the Galaxy*, and DC's *The New 52: Futures End*. "In 2012 we also participated in a unique countywide poetry event called *O, Miami*, merging the world of comic books and poetry. It was a very interesting event that garnered tons of attention and costumed attendees."

Aside from great customer service, the store offers a unique subscription service that guarantees a copy of new releases to each member. Additionally, if the store does not carry an item a customer is seeking, Jorge will find a way to procure it. They are not limited to just comics, but also carry collectibles and vintage toys, offering visitors a blast from the past.

Keeping the store open has not been an easy feat, especially with the advent of technology. "It would not be the same if we placed items for sale online," Jorge says. "Nothing beats the experience of coming into the store and seeing what we have or uncovering something new and cool or simply the fact that you are coming into a store and touching the item in your hands and interacting with people. And believe it or not, people still like to read the physical copy. Something just does not feel right when you are reading it from a PDF file. You just have to come into the store to see it for yourself."

A.C.'s ICEES

DAVID T. KENNEDY PARK

2600 S. BAYSHORE DR. • COCONUT GROVE, FL 33146

Miami's Food Truck Godfather

For a city that is hot year-round, one would expect it to be littered with frozen lemonade spots, but the opposite is true. Only a handful of brands offer the icy treat, like Toby's and Del's, and A.C.'s Icees remains the most sought after and iconic. Located in David T. Kennedy Park's parking lot, parking can be tough, but that does not keep patrons of the thirty-plus-year frozen lemonade institution away. Locals also love the park, as it overlooks Biscayne Bay and includes a dog park and an outdoor gym.

A.C. is short for Allan Cohen, the owner. Disappointed by the corporate world, he moved to Miami to live a life that most only dream of. Coconut Grove was his favorite vacation spot growing up. Originally from the cold tundra of Michigan, he opened shop in 1978 after he noticed that fellow park-goers had to walk blocks for refreshment after exercising or simply being in the hot Miami weather. The closest establishment is the Starbucks at the Monty's Raw Bar complex, 0.3 mile away.

For Cohen, life is a park. In between serving customers, he chills in his park chair, oftentimes playing Frisbee, his favorite sport, with local passersby. On May 26, 1982, the *Miami News* featured a great image of the iconic owner playing Frisbee. He is usually in a T-shirt and shorts, with his wild blond mane in full splendor.

Cohen keeps it old-school. He operates out of a converted white General Motors step van that dons yellow awnings and a bright hot dog umbrella over its backside. The food truck has no phone and Cohen does not own a computer, much less an e-mail address, but the operation has survived decades without it, making it a great example of grassroots business that survives on the loyalty of its patrons and word of mouth. The location at Kennedy Park is near Ransom Everglades School, and the icees are extremely popular with its students, so much so that a group created a Facebook page for A.C.'s Icees with general information. At sixty years old, Allan's nephew Richard now runs the operation full-time, but you can still find him milling about a couple of times a week.

The history books show evidence of food trucks as early as 1691 in New York in the form of street vendors selling food from pushcarts. Ice cream trucks made their appearance in the fifties, and the roach coach appeared on construction sites in the sixties. Miami is no stranger to the phenomena. A.C.'s Icees is considered to be the grandfather of Miami food trucks, being the first to receive a mobile concession permit from the city. Throughout Miami it is equally easy to find street vendors peddling items from fruits and vegetables to water, sunglasses, and even shrimp. If A.C.'s Icees was the first of its kind, Gastropod and Latin Burger heralded the second generation. These days, food trucks are all the rage, and there are at least fifty on the Miami food truck list.

In 2008 a party was thrown in Cohen's honor. To commemorate his thirty years in business, the city placed and named a stone seating area close to the truck's usual spot in Kennedy Park. "A.C.'s Icees is historic," says Sef Gonzalez, aka Burger Beast, Miami's foremost burger expert and writer. "I do not think many people [outside the Coconut Grove area, that is] realize that. As a food truck connoisseur, I am embarrassed to say that it took me a long time to finally try it, but once I did, I was hooked. Cohen and his truck offer a glimpse into the area's past—when hippies ruled Peacock Park and a laid-back lifestyle was the norm."

Open daily from 11 a.m. to 6 p.m., Cohen has the diligence and work ethic that most people do not possess. The truck is always there at 11 a.m., without fail, no matter rain or shine, cold or heat. The only time A.C.'s Icees is not open is during a hurricane. A cartoon version of his face is plastered on both the truck and the cups. Cohen sells frosted icees in lemonade, cherry, and piña colada flavors and fresh-squeezed grapefruit and orange juices as well as water, iced tea, and sodas. The piña colada even has whole chunks of pineapple.

For mega brain freeze, opt for the 24-ounce at six bucks. If you are hungry, he also sells Sabrett's hot dogs on fresh steamed buns with cooked onions and spicy brown mustard. The business still operates as cash-only.

So, what makes an excellent frozen lemonade? It must be generous in portion; its flavor, the right amount of sweet and tart, and its consistency, both sippable and spoonable. In Miami, it is blasphemy to decree 7-Eleven the top dog in the frozen drink game. A.C.'s Icees is a way of life in this town.

ALLEN'S DRUG STORE

4000 S. RED RD. • MIAMI, FL 33155

(305) 666-8581 • MYPHARMACY.COM

A Spoonful of Chili Helps the Medicine Go Down

*A*llen's Drug Store is a survivor. Cue that old Destiny's Child song now. Like many other stories that intertwine in this book, Allen's is located at the edge of the same shopping center that once housed Beehive Natural Foods. Despite its close proximity, Allen's is not located in the confines of the CVS Pharmacy space, even though it is only a few feet away. Hallelujah, a landmark in Miami was saved! CVS will move in as the third pharmacy in the intersection, but neither CVS nor Walgreens offer the kitsch, nostalgia, or service and, in some cases, the products that Allen's does. While many fear for the future of Allen's, its owners and the history books predict that this one is here to stay for a long while. Well, that is, unless Duane Reade decides to expand into Florida territory. Then all bets are off.

Like many other stores and industries in Miami, independent drugstores and pharmacies have gone the way of the dinosaur. The definition of an independent drugstore is one that is independent from the large retailers and usually pharmacist owned. This is true for Allen's, which is now owned and operated by Al Collazo, a pharmacist himself.

In a *Miami News* article from March 1981, Herb Rau called the store "the kind of place that hides its prescription counter amongst a maze of sundry goods." It is true; they stock just about everything, but have found a niche for themselves in the medical supplies business. Allen's has not changed much since the beginning. It is an

old-fashioned drugstore, with a Formica-countertop lunch counter and a watch repair counter. Regulars are a must and frequent it on a sometimes-daily basis. For the old-timers, it is a nostalgic spot to get together with friends and reminisce about chocolate-dipped sodas and nickel ice cream cones. It is also a neighborhood place, the type where everyone knows your name and your favorite food item. For the younger crowd, it offers a tangible glimpse into the past that is not in the form of a museum.

Located on the famous Bird Road, Woolworths and B-Thrifty also existed nearby and posed stiff competition to Allen's a few decades ago. The corner store originally opened as the new branch of Breeding Drugstore in the late forties to early fifties. Originally from South Carolina, John Allen Sr. became the pharmacy manager for Breeding Drugstore in 1951. In 1954 he purchased the store and converted it into Allen's Drug Store, along with some light remodeling and expansion. Allen had moved to West Palm Beach in the twenties and studied pharmacy by working up the ladder in various pharmacies. In the eighties, Al Collazo acquired the company.

For decades the soda fountain inside of Allen's was Picnics. In 2011, due to a possible location move for another historical legend,

S&S Diner opened a second location in place of Picnics. Eventually, the official move for S&S Diner from downtown never happened, and the Allen's location was sold to different owners. The S&S Diner at Allen's is more commonly referred to as The Diner, even though S&S's red lights shine on the pharmacy's exterior. They serve breakfast, lunch, and dinner. A little-known secret, their banana pudding is one of the best in town. And despite all the changes, they are still famous for their chili, which will only set you back $3.95. Other comfort foods include Salisbury steak, meat loaf, and country-fried steak. Perusing through newspapers of yore, you will find ads and articles touting the chili.

There are interesting articles out there about the phenomenon of independent drugstores that are still open and profitable. In 2011 Todd Marks, senior editor of *Consumer Reports*, said, "We found that the independents made fewer errors, offered swifter service at the pharmacy counter, and were more likely to have medications ready for pick up when promised." In March 2012 *Businessweek* followed up with an article titled "End of Days for Independent Pharmacies?" in which Karen E. Klein found that about half of independent pharmacies are located in cities with populations of 20,000 or fewer. Allen's is dodging that last statistic, successfully operating in a city of 40,000.

And while there are many benefits to the independents—exceptional customer service, timeliness, heart, nostalgia, one-of-a-kind products—prices tend to be more expensive. In the old days, a prescription would set you back no more than a buck and change; now it is upwards of $15. Either way, ask any customer at the store if that matters, and they will note that they come for the experience and would rather pay the extra for care and quality.

Most recently Allen's became a hot spot for political debate about the country's changing health-care laws. In early 2014 Joe Biden stopped by to nosh on some food at S&S Diner and talk about the Affordable Care Act.

ARBETTER'S HOT DOGS

8747 SW 40TH ST. • MIAMI, FL 33165

(305) 207-0555 • ARBETTERS.COM

"There Are None Better!"

*A*rbetter's Hot Dogs is Miami's answer to Nathan's Hot Dogs and a source of American pride in the heart of the Cuban suburb of Westchester. An old-school favorite, the hot dog restaurant thrives on the love and support of the local community. Through that community dedication, it has won *Miami New Times*'s "Best Of" awards twice, in 2006 and 2009. The 2006 award write-up featured an interesting statistic that holds the key to its continued success and longevity: "The National Hot Dog and Sausage Council estimates Americans will eat more than seven billion little red tubes of 'specially selected meat trimmings' between Memorial Day and Labor Day weekends."

Robert "Bob" Arbetter may have passed away in 2003, but the legacy of his restaurant, Arbetter's Hot Dogs, continues as strong today as when it opened in 1962. A Boston native and hard-core sports fanatic, Bob initially came to Miami to attend the University of Miami. Boston has a strong hot dog culture, and he quickly noticed that Miami lacked not only a penchant for the comfort food, but also a decent dog vendor or restaurant. He set out to fill the void, fulfilling his lifetime dream of owning and operating a hot dog restaurant.

Arbetter's occupied a few locations before settling into the restaurant's current home on Bird Road in 1972. Bob left Boston to get away from the city and liked Westchester much better than downtown or even Miami Beach for its hometown feel and close-knit community. The restaurant continues to be popular with high school students

from nearby schools such as St. Brendan, Christopher Columbus, Coral Park, and Southwest High School, who use it as their afternoon hangout spot. Many of these students grew up going to Arbetter's with their parents and are now going on their own, continuing the family tradition of customers, which the restaurant promotes.

Bob sold the restaurant a number of times to travel and enjoy the retired life, but he could not stay away and ultimately repurchased it each time. Others just did not know how to run it like the Arbetters could. "He loved the restaurant so much. He was there seven days a week with a smile on his face, preparing hot dogs and entertaining customers," says Andrew, Bob's grandson.

Bob was the ultimate sports fanatic. No joke, he loved Larry Bird, Bob Cousy, and the Celtics. There are even two signs at the restaurant that read: "Free Boston Baked Beans the Day after the Red Sox Win the World Series" and "Free Refills This Week When You Say I Love Larry Bird or Bob Cousy." In 2004, 2007, and 2013 the Red Sox won the World Series and the restaurant was true to its word, celebrating with fans and dishing out free servings of Boston baked beans. The 2004 win was bittersweet, as Bob passed away one year shy of the first big win since 1918. On the basketball side, Miami folks should not be worried, since he loved the Miami Heat as passionately as his Celtics. His son and daughter, David and Jill, run the store with the help of Jill's sons, Andrew and Casey. Andrew, in his early twenties, is now the unofficial spokesperson for the restaurant.

Arbetter's continues to be a reminder of old-school Miami. The small place, clad in red and yellow with seventies-style wood paneling, is no larger than a modest trailer, seating twenty people snuggly inside and about a dozen more on the outdoor patio. Celtics memorabilia line the walls, and the open kitchen fills the air with sausage goodness. The menu is simple: hot dogs, corn dogs, fries, and sodas. The restaurant employs a unique ordering system: A hot dog with mustard and onions is an M.O. Dog, a dog with chili and onions is a C.O. Dog, and so on.

Aside from the hot dogs, Arbetter's is most known for its chili. Made with meat and no beans, it is served as a condiment for the hot dog and is a secret recipe from Bob's wife's immigrant Italian family. Different from other hot dog empires, the dogs at Arbetter's are boiled, not grilled, and a mix of beef and pork. They also do not toast the rolls. Nothing on the menu is more than $4 and only cash is accepted. The restaurant's mission, menu, and interiors have not changed much either. The menu's only changes in the past fifty-two years have been the removal of the hamburger and the addition of the corn dog, which is also a popular item. When was the last time you had a corn dog?

"My grandfather loved doing little tricks while cooking to entertain his customers," Andrew says. "This is more than a family store; it is a community store. He remembered everyone's names and loved the generations of families that would come in. My grandfather was an old-school guy. He would wear wraps on his pants to prevent them from getting dirty, along with a white T-shirt. Ironically, his T-shirt was always dirty at the end of the day, but there was no convincing him otherwise. He went through a lot of white T-shirts. Life on Bird Road is great, and I would not have it any other way. As far as the rest of historic Bird Road, I love Frankie's Pizza; it is my favorite pizza in town. Most everyone [business owners] on Bird Road knows and supports each other and everyone knew my grandfather. There is only one Arbetter's (And it is worth the trip!)."

AUSTIN BURKE

2601 NW SIXTH AVE. • MIAMI, FL 33127

(305) 576-2714 • AUSTINBURKEFL.NET

It Is a Boys' Club

*A*ustin Burke's famous jingle goes like this: "Suits, suits, and more suits, come see little ole Burkie, Austin Burke suits."

In the land of fashion, women tend to dominate the scene, and as the years have passed, the world of traditional menswear has been taken over by the big department stores, losing its old-world charm and character in the shuffle. When Austin Burke opened in 1945, Gatti's Restaurant and the National Hotel were all the rage, and Dressel's Dairy and MacArthur's Dairy still made home deliveries. Fast-forward sixty-nine years, and the store continues strong with Austin Burke's son, Barry Burke, at the helm along with his cousin, Kenny Sager. These days, stores like Austin Burke are one of a kind and deserve attention.

"For many, suits are an everyday norm; for others, it is a once in a blue moon, torturous event," says Sager. "Either way, the art of picking and purchasing a suit is made infinitely better at Austin Burke. Guys, here is some simple but essential advice: The most important part of a suit is its fit, and every suit, no matter how great it fits, requires at least a little bit of tailoring. Color is next; you may be walking around in a black suit when you were meant to be in navy blue. Those little details are what take you to the next level."

Austin Burke moved from Philadelphia in 1945 and opened the store shortly thereafter on Lincoln Road. In the fifties the store did heavy advertising with Gilbert and Tormey Inc., a popular trend of the *Mad Men* days. Burke was a well-known announcer and was locally famous for his comedic television and radio commercials to promote

the store, where he would strip off layer upon layer of sports coats. He was a jovial man and referred to himself as Little Ole Burkie, even though he was a little fat man. Those who knew him say he was as one of a kind as the store, a top-notch gentleman.

In the sixties the family moved the business to Miami's Wynwood neighborhood, then known as Miami's Fashion District. A heavily industrial neighborhood, one can still see remnants of this in the abandoned manufacturing buildings and warehouse clothing stores on Seventh Street. The neighborhood dates back to the thirties, when New Yorkers came down to live in Miami during the boom, relocating their manufacturing businesses to the area—clearly these things were much easier back then. With the mass influx of immigrants in the sixties, Miami's Fashion District was ground zero for jobs. In the seventies the manufacturing industry moved overseas, and the facilities were converted into retail stores. The district became a discount retailer's paradise, selling quality merchandise. In the eighties it was easy to find authentic designer handbags like Chanel and Dior for as little as $30.

Austin Burke is housed in a 20,000-square-foot space and offers quality men's clothing at bargain prices in a warehouse-style setting. They offer fine suits from business wear to tuxedos by designers like

Ralph Lauren, Canali, and Armani in three-button, two-button, single-breasted, double-breasted, and linen styles. They even sell shoes and, of course, all the accoutrements to a designer suit like ties and collared shirts, which line the walls from floor to ceiling. Returning to Sager's important point about a well-fitted suit, they employ tailors to make sure that all suits fit the customers to a T. Mostly of Italian and Greek origin, all tailors work in-house. Austin Burke procures both their merchandise and their employees internationally and from

Vintage Spot
PETE'S SUNILAND BARBER SHOP: EST. 1956

A political watering hole and old-school boys' club, Pete's has been providing top-quality cuts and shaves since the fifties. With memorabilia on the walls and old-timey decor, it is a step back in time. Talk to any of the barbers and you can learn about Miami's history, including the famous Suniland Shopping Center shootings of the eighties. Hey, sometimes tourists need a haircut, too. Skip the Supercuts and opt for a true Miami experience.

11505 S. Dixie Hwy.; (305) 251-5893

New York, ensuring high-quality product and service and, above all, fantastic fit.

Even famous people love the Burke. The store has outfitted movies like *The Devil Wears Prada* and television shows like *Miami Vice*. Magic Johnson, Burt Reynolds, Donny Johnson, Lou Ferrigno, Shaquille O'Neal, and most of the Miami Heat basketball team are clients. Regular ole folks like him, too. Local favorites Danny Serfer of Blue Collar and Joshua Marcus of Josh's Deli are clients as well. "I had heard the commercials for years growing up down here, but never checked it out until recently when I had to get a black suit for a wedding," says Serfer. "I was so impressed with the service, quality, and value that I have gone back a bunch since then—sometimes to buy, sometimes just to chat with the character that is Kenny. Turns out he [Sager] is also a fan of Blue Collar Restaurant and we hit it off. Few businesses have been around Miami as long as Austin Burke, and I hope to be a cool Miami guy like him one day."

Austin Burke continues as an anchor for the neighborhood, and its high visibility remains when driving on I-95. The large green lettering flanked by an oversize shamrock is hard to miss. The neighborhood is experiencing yet another renaissance, and as it continues to grow and change, the store will remain as a window into the past, not only in style, but also in service. "Like wine, our store only gets finer and finer with age," says Sager.

BEEHIVE NATURAL FOODS

6490 SW 40TH ST. • MIAMI, FL 33155

(305) 663-3360

Keeping Miami Au Naturel

It was the mid-nineties when I first stopped eating meat, and back then it was all side dishes and salads," says Lauren "Lolo" Reskin of the local veg scene. "There were always a few places that were kosher or catered to hippies where you could find some better options, but a veg entree was basically unheard of. Since then a ton of places have opened up that cater to people who are veg or just want to eat healthier. Sublime in Fort Lauderdale is an upscale vegan restaurant that has been open for ages now. In Miami we have Choices Café; smaller chains like Evos and Yard House serving faux meat; a fully vegan bakery, Bunnie Cakes; and just many more options across the board. Every new 'foodie' place I have been to lately has had more than enough selections for a solid and interesting meatless meal."

When Robert "Bob" Penna opened his store in 1980, there were a lot more health food stores around. Many eventually went out of business as the larger natural and organic chain-grocery stores opened. But while there were many stores like Beehive Natural Foods when it opened, there were not many restaurants that catered to vegans and vegetarians. Now, everything is more balanced and Miami has truly come into its own.

Penna loves telling the story of his journey. He never liked traditional medicine. At twenty-three years old, he was in fairly good shape; he exercised a lot and ate the typical American diet, but he suffered from allergies, skin rashes, hemorrhoids, hypoglycemia, and had problems with his eyes. He had been going to doctors for years, but nothing cured what ailed him. He had heard about natural remedies and decided to give them a try. He tried zinc for his skin rashes; he actually opened up the capsule and spread the powder all over his legs. The rashes healed up immediately. He went on to try vitamin C for his bleeding gums, and it also worked. Finally, he tried vitamin A for his eyes and to boost his concentration and, voila, it was a miracle. He was converted and decided to become a nutritionist.

Penna is now sixty-one, but he is stronger than ever and shows no signs of slowing down. He notes that the store is his doctor. "I like what I do, and I offer nutritional advice and customer service to my clients that remained loyal and moved with the store," he says. "I am kind of like a bartender, but instead of drinks, I sling herbs, vitamins, and minerals. I like the social aspect of it, and we are giving people something that will make them feel better."

In 2013 the store was on the verge of going to vintage heaven, as the strip mall in which it was previously located was sold to CVS Pharmacy—a ridiculous move that has many in Miami shaking their heads, as this new addition would make it the third pharmacy on the block. There already is a Walgreens across the street and stalwart Allen's Drug Store next door. Other long-running establishments with simple names like Karate, Red Bird Shoe Repair, Whole Sale Antique Center, and the Dry Cleaning were Beehive's neighbors at the now-defunct plaza. Like siblings going to foster homes, they are all being separated, some even closing permanently.

The new Beehive, located only seven blocks west from the original location, is two and half times bigger and offers a fresh beginning and greater visibility. Chef Carlos Schicchi is still there, too. The Brazilian chef, who has a cult following, subleases space from Penna and operates a cafe inside the store. Serving up to 180 meals a day, the cafe with its many regulars feels like a secret club with its own language and rules. Most everybody raves about the Rain Forest juice, an unlikely combination of carrot juice, lime juice, avocado, banana, and ginger. The menu is unlike any other in town, featuring items like lentils, tofu, seitan, and tempeh, and does not use dairy, eggs, or animal products, turning unknown or alien products into creative familiar dishes like wheat empanadas, tofu picadillo, spinach cakes, and lasagna. For those with a less adventurous palate, there are fresh fruit, brown rice casserole, kale chips, and vegan cheese.

The cafe is unique because it conforms to the changing diets of the day, from the South Beach Diet to Weight Watchers and everything in between. They also sell dehydrated crackers and raw fruit pie. Elsewhere, you will find protein bars, soymilk, and vitamins: The store's biggest seller is liquid probiotic to aid with digestive and respiratory problems. At 16 ounces, it sells for $13.95. Another best seller at the store is the Life Extension Enhanced FernBlock with Sendara, which is essentially sunscreen in a pill. Meant to be used as a complement to sunscreen, it does not contain animal products, sugar, and, in many cases, gluten.

Many who have been around for a while may remember the craze of high tea in the late eighties. A *Miami News* article from October 20, 1986, highlights how the craze led to some buzz for the local store. Penna says it turned out to be much ado about nothing. When word leaked out that the Peruvian tea contained traces of cocaine, swarms of drug enforcement officers, users, and the media scrambled to confiscate, brew, and report on this phenomenon. "NBC came down from New York and everything—but they never showed it on TV. I guess they thought it was not such a big story after all," Penna says.

THE BILTMORE HOTEL

1200 ANASTASIA AVE. • MIAMI, FL 33134

(855) 311-6903 • BILTMOREHOTEL.COM

Old-World Glamour

The Biltmore is unlike any other hotel in Miami. Located in the heart of the posh suburban city of Coral Gables, it stands as an example of old-world glamour in the otherwise bustling City Beautiful. The alluring building set in the architectural style of Mediterranean Revival entices visitors long before they even step foot through its doors. The hotel's centerpiece, its center tower, modeled after the Giralda Tower in Seville, Spain, once stood as the tallest building in Coral Gables and teases passersby with its peak that looms above the old banyan trees that cover the city's roads.

Coral Gables was the dream of George Merrick, and the hotel was his masterpiece, the one thing that tied all of the Mediterranean influences together, offering not only lodging, but also a central entertainment hub. It is a timeless dream, with hand-painted ceilings, lush courtyards, fountains, balconies, marble columns, terrazzo and travertine floors, and the grand lobby with various plush and luxurious seating options and a massive 8-foot birdcage with precious birds chirping away.

The hotel opened in January of 1926 to great fanfare in the middle of the Prohibition era. Opening night was the social event of the year, attracting socialites from all over the country, especially those from the Northeast, riding down on special trains marked "Miami Biltmore Special" to attend the party. An estimated 1,500 guests attended the magnificent event, which included booze, the foxtrot, and a lavish menu of turtle soup, veal with foie gras, and Strawberries Romanoff. This would set the tone for the hotel, which quickly became a regular

spot for Al Capone, Bing Crosby, Judy Garland, and the Vanderbilt family, along with presidents, dignitaries, dukes, and duchesses.

The Everglades Suite, less formally known as the Al Capone Suite, was named after the notorious gangster. It is said that Capone owned the suite for a period of time. In 1929 another mobster, Thomas "Fatty" Walsh, was murdered at the hotel. The Biltmore always managed to stay in the limelight, whether for its beauty or its murders.

In the twenties, thirties, and early forties, it was normal for hotels to offer a robust schedule of events, as they served as the entertainment hubs for the city. The Biltmore hosted a mixture of galas, fashion shows, aquatic shows, big band variety shows, and alligator wrestlers, a local favorite. More unique were the gondola rides, fox hunting, and private helicopter rides. Gondola rides, you ask? Gondoliers would transport guests to the hotel's private beach down the canals of Coral Gables. But those were gauche times, and that private beach no longer exists.

Like the Raleigh Hotel, the Biltmore has an iconic pool that is one of the largest in the country. In the twenties and thirties, a lot of synchronized swimming took place in the pool. Even Tarzan himself,

Johnny Weissmuller, swam in Coral Gables; not only did he hang out at the public Venetial Pool, he was also a swimming instructor at the Biltmore pool.

The Nat Gubbins is a popular cocktail originally featured in Helen Muir's book *The Biltmore: Beacon for Miami*, which captures the detailed history of one of Miami's most famous hotels. The Nat Gubbins is a lost cocktail that was birthed at the hotel's Cascades Bar and named after a London columnist who traveled to the Biltmore for a writing assignment shortly after its opening. The aperitif drink is half port, half brandy, served with a twist of lemon and no ice. Unfortunately, the drink died off with its inventor; it has not been served since those early decades and lives on only in memory.

When the hotel first opened, it claimed two golf courses, but now there is only one (the other became the nearby Riviera Country Club). The Biltmore Golf Course is one of the best in the country and popular with golfers of all kinds. According to historians, celebrities like Babe Ruth, Johnny Weissmuller, Bill Clinton, and Tiger Woods have played on the greens. The famous Donald Ross designed the impressive course.

Like many other hotels in the city, the Biltmore was used as an infirmary and training facility for soldiers during World War II. It was formally known as the Army Air Forces Regional Hospital and then remained an arm of the nearby University of Miami School of Medicine. The hotel sat empty between 1968 and 1983, which preserved

Vintage Spot
miami river inn: est. 1910

Listed on the National Register of Historic Places, this is one of Miami's oldest lodging establishments. The yellow and green cottages are reminiscent of Miami's pioneer days, and their interiors are outfitted with antiques in bright colors and more Miami style.

118 SW South River Dr.; (305) 325-0045; miamiriverinn.com

its integrity, its features, and possibly its ghosts. Many visitors to the hotel note that it is haunted, mainly from the era when it served as a hospital.

After a big push and lots of elbow grease, the eighties brought renewed hope and brilliance to the Biltmore, with a massive restoration project that took four years and millions of dollars. In 1987, sixty-one years after it originally opened, a historic dinner was held to commemorate the reopening of the hotel. The dinner was a true nod to history, as the hotel served items from the original opening decades prior, but this time the booze was legal. Like its past, the event was the social highlight of the season, but drew much less crowds than the first time around, at around 600 individuals.

The restaurants are as much of an attraction as the hotel itself, the most famous being Palme d'Or, helmed by award-winning chef Philippe Ruiz. The hotel's Sunday brunch is a one-of-a-kind experience out of a foodie's dreams, including everything from caviar and sushi to prime aged meats and international cheeses, with an abundance of stations and options. Afternoon high tea accompanied by a harpist is also offered in the lobby.

BIRD BOWL

9275 SW 40TH ST. • MIAMI, FL 33165

(305) 221-1221 • BIRDBOWL.COM

Bowlers Do It in the Alley

*B*ird Bowl is located in a strip mall on Bird Road adjacent to El Rey de las Fritas, an outpost of the original Cuban hamburger joint. It is also on the same famed road as Frankie's Pizza and Arbetter's Hot Dogs and across the street from Yesterday and Today Records, all making for a fantastic jaunt through old Miami. Following the unspoken tradition, one cannot visit Bird Bowl without a stop at Frankie's or Arbetter's.

Bird Bowl is a bowler's bowling alley, clad with fluorescent lighting, blue-checkered floors, an aquatic backdrop behind the pins, neon bowling shoes, and the sweaty smell of victory. One that even Jeffrey Lebowski aka The Dude would visit if *The Big Lebowski* took a trip to Miami. As opposed to Strike Miami, Lucky Strike, and Splitsville, which are boutique bowling alleys, Bird Bowl offers traditional bowling. The aforementioned boutique bowling alleys are not official lanes and therefore are not used by sanctioned leagues.

When Bird Bowl was built, it was the largest bowling alley in the South. It continues to be an example for large bowling alleys at sixty lanes. Like most other entertainment palaces, Bird Bowl offers birthday parties, a greasy snack bar that even serves breakfast, and karaoke. It is not trendy, but it is still fun and that is all that matters when bowling. In a separate section, the billiards and arcade offer a more intimate vibe. The sixteen billiard tables and classic video games and air hockey in the arcade are a huge draw for customers, who will trek to the alley exclusively for the games.

As the only old-school bowling alley left in town, it is important to recall the early days of Miami's bowling landscape, which history shows was one of the best in the country. In 2005 Dick Evans, a bowling journalist, wrote a well-researched and greatly informative piece on the scene, which lasted from 1956 to 1991. At its high point, there were a total of eighteen bowling centers in Miami and the city hosted such great tournaments as the BPAA National All-Star Tournament, the Women's U.S. Open, and the Tournament of the Americas, among others. In a May 20, 1959 article in the *Miami News*, a survey of bowlers concluded the following: The Greater Miami Bowling Association had 100 leagues and 3,500 members in 1956, and by 1959 the number had jumped to 320 leagues and 12,000 members.

At the height of its popularity, bowling leagues were plentiful and popular tournaments such as the Tangerine Classic and the Sheehan Buick Classic graced the city's lanes. Daily newspapers were awash with stories about bowling leagues, tournaments, and scores, each league with a fervent following much like the modern-day Miami Heat fans. Battles between men and women were also extremely popular.

Bird Bowl faced strong competition from Bowling Palace, Airport Lanes, Coliseum Lanes, and Cloverleaf Lanes. Historically, bowling centers were built on the fringes of town. This was not the case in Miami, however, as one of the most popular lanes, the Miami Recreation Lanes, was located in the heart of downtown.

Similar to other establishments featured in this book, Bird Bowl is one of the few original spots remaining from the glory days of the fifties. Opened in 1956 by Albert Johnson, the alley has been in business for more than half a century, and it's safe to say they know what bowling is all about. Having owned a number of bowling establishments in Chicago, Johnson came from Illinois in 1955 with tons of bowling experience in the hopes of establishing a successful site here. He lived in Coral Gables, but not much else is known about him other than the fact that he preferred to go by Al.

After Al's untimely death, his son continued managing the operation before selling it to a private partnership in 1981. Major renovations kicked in after the sale, including the upgrade to modern bowling technology with the additions of automatic scoring and a sound system. Prior to the installation of the sound system, bands would play on a contract basis. Can you imagine bowling to the sounds of soul and funk? The last of Bird Bowl's traditional competitors, Don Carter's, closed in 2006.

One of the top dogs at the alley, Theresa Ore, has been around the longest at approximately sixteen years. She says, "Once Al's son left, Bird Bowl lost ties to the original owners. I am not really sure where the family went. No one around here, not even me, was around to see it. It was all before our time. But, the original values and the sense of community that they instilled have never gone away. The bowling pins out front were put in five to seven years ago and they are extremely popular. They really spruced up the tired facade. They are especially popular with kids that like to climb them."

CAPTAIN'S TAVERN RESTAURANT & SEAFOOD MARKET

9625 S. DIXIE HWY. • MIAMI, FL 33156
(305) 666-5979 • CAPTAINSTAVERNMIAMI.COM

A Seventies-Style Fish House

*H*ere are some things you should immediately know about Captain's Tavern: It is one of the longest-running restaurants in South Dade. They do not take reservations, and you will wait in line. During peak dining hours, this means a wait of up to two hours. Sound familiar? Yes, these wait times are reminiscent of those at Joe's Stone Crab. This is interesting to point out because the two restaurants are located on two different ends of the spectrum (in offerings, decor, clientele, location, and mission), but both are equally successful in their own respect.

A little known secret is that Captain's has one of the most extensive and best-priced wine lists in town. With over 600 bottles on the list, not only are the wines carefully chosen, but they are also priced at store value and not marked up like in most restaurants. Chef Cindy Hutson, a local food pioneer, recommends the Maine lobster here. Every Tuesday night is lobster night with two-for-one lobster. They serve over 3,000 customers a week and go through thousands of pounds of fish and shellfish weekly. And they serve good fish, everything from fresh hog snapper, Everglades yellowtail, tuna, dolphin and grouper to scallops, oysters, Florida lobster, and shrimp. The restaurant's menu is greatly influenced by the owner's wife, Audrey, who was born and raised in Jamaica; you will find touches of the Caribbean mixed in, boding well for Miami's spice-loving palate.

Captain's decor is stuck in the seventies, and many have criticized the restaurant's owners for this. Like Fox's Sherron Inn just up

Vintage Spot

GARCIA'S SEAFOOD GRILLE & FISH MARKET: EST. 1966

For locals and tourists alike, this is the first stop after leaving Miami International Airport. Located on the Miami River, it is an open-air restaurant and market that offers a great ambience with scenic views and fresh seafood.

398 NW North River Dr.; (305) 375-0765; garciasmiami.com

the road, the restaurant is cavelike since there are no windows, but unlike its compatriot, this is a bright space inside, with tons of yellow lighting, nautical paraphernalia, dark wood paneling, and blue-lit fish aquariums. As for the criticism, the owner does not mind. He is there to serve food and has coined the decor "early Depression chic." The restaurant opened in 1971, and having not undergone any renovations since then, it makes sense that it still sports a seventies style. In a place like Miami with its rat race for modernity, Captain's offers a slice of kitschy cool. And the anchor outside offers a neat welcome.

Located in the same neighborhood as Mainzer's German Deli and the aforementioned Fox's Sherron Inn, the restaurant is one for the locals. While it has been raved about by *Gourmet* magazine and frequented by celebrities like Betty Ford and Yogi Berra, it is the locals who keep this place beating. It attracts an interesting crowd as well, probably the largest gathering of non-Hispanic folks in the area.

Bill Bowers is the mastermind behind the restaurant. Now in his eighties, he is still running the show. Back in the seventies, when he got his start, there was not much else around, but the restaurant offered a new life and new options to the area. Many of the same customers from those early days are still regulars. Word of mouth has really been the great driver for this restaurant.

Originally from New England and a former Edward's Produce delivery driver, Bowers wanted to bring the same enthusiasm for fresh fish with an emphasis on local favorites to the sleepy town of what is now known as Pinecrest. Everyone thought he was crazy, but he persevered and now gets the last laugh. Prior to being a restaurant, the space housed a US Post Office. Located off the main artery of US 1, it is tucked away in a shopping center and sometimes hard to find, but this does not keep folks away. The *Miami New Times* once wrote: "Though it is hidden in the shadows off South Dixie Highway, there is hardly ever an empty table at Captain's Tavern." Also located adjacent to the restaurant is Captain's Tavern Seafood Market, open most days until 6 p.m. It offers everything the fish lover needs to replicate the Captain's experience at home, sans the seventies kitsch.

And in case you were wondering, Bill Bowers was once indeed a seafaring captain.

CAULEY SQUARE HISTORIC RAILROAD VILLAGE

22400 OLD DIXIE HWY. • MIAMI, FL 33170

(305) 258-3543 • CAULEYSQUARE.COM

A Glimpse of Old South Florida

Although it is a tropical, laid-back paradise, one rarely associates Miami with bohemian villages. In fact, all of the local options in this category can be counted on one hand: Coconut Grove, Española Way, and Cauley Square Historic Railroad Village. Different from its counterparts, Cauley Square offers an experience unlike any other, with a real glimpse into the world of old South Florida. The historic village consists of twelve stores, six gardens, and three restaurants—the Tea Room, the Village Chalet, and Latin Corner, which specializes in Colombian-style hot dogs and homemade shakes in tropical flavors. The shops are equally unique, selling everything from birds and flowers to art, ceramics, jewelry, and handmade products worthy of Etsy standards, all the stuff of dreams for vintage and craft lovers.

Cauley Square is home to the Antique & Classic Car Show and, most recently, the new home of the Renaissance Festival, fitting right in with its world of knights, pirates, and turkey legs. It is also a popular stop on the Redland Riot Road Rallye, created by native rum expert and preservation enthusiast Robert Burr; it is a self-guided tour through Miami's deep south, where history abounds. Once you pass The Falls mall and the general Pinecrest area, you enter a world stuck in time, with pockets of eccentric, historic locations such as the Florida Pioneer Museum, Historic Homestead, Knaus Berry Farm, and Robert Is Here.

Spanning 10 acres, Cauley Square is located off US 1 in the town of Goulds in Homestead and is made up of clapboard-style cottages, which serve as homes for the stores and restaurants of the Village. In the early 1900s, Miami's beginnings played out near the mouth of Biscayne Bay in the heart of what is now known as downtown Miami, but farther south, the rural town of Goulds also boomed. Henry Flagler's Florida East Coast Railway reached the area in 1903. William H. Cauley, a local pioneer farmer and owner of the 10 acres surrounding the railroad center, built Cauley Square that same year to increase the population of the town. Historically the cottages served as homes for the workers of Flagler's railway. Additionally, Flagler used the village as his shipping hub for tomatoes, which he would send north in the winter. Cauley Square claims to be the last railroad village in Florida and one of the last in the century. At the time, the Village also housed a bar and grill, offices, and warehouses, but it was not always quaint—typical of a pioneer town, stories of booze and brothels were rampant.

Despite the Great Depression and World War II, the area remained rural for decades, until the residential and commercial boom of the early 2000s drastically changed the landscape. Now, there are more strip malls than agriculture. Cauley Square began

a steady decline, and it was condemned by the county and slated for demolition. Enter Mary Ann Ballard, an interior designer and preservationist, who set out to save Cauley Square along with her husband. It was her idea to bring more independent and craft businesses to the Village. She wanted to provide local residents a place to meet and relax.

Ballard opened the Tea Room in 1979. Filled with delicate china, crystal, and lace, it is what every little girl imagines a real teahouse to be. The quaint restaurant is divided into different rooms, which are adorned with cabinets, teapots, china sets, stained glass, lamps, an ancient stove, and a piano. The famous Tea Room serves a variety of hot and cold teas as well as delicious sweet treats from German chocolate and coconut cakes to apple-cranberry harvest pie.

A *Boca Raton News* article from September 4, 1983, offers a rare interview with Mary Ann Ballard: "Most of the shops, she confesses, are operated by people who have never been in business. There is no hard sell and an aura of neighborliness pervades. A visit here differs from other villages of yesteryear because of the indigenous flora along the village paths. Everything here is original—non-hybrid hibiscus, Poinciana, yucca-type plants, rare ferns, gumbo-limbo, avocado, lime and mango trees."

Honey Chalmers's Today's Collectibles antiques shop also has its place in history. Her shop has been in operation since the eighties, and her cottage served as one of Flagler's many homes. You can find Art Deco lamps salvaged from Biscayne Boulevard's McAllister Hotel, one of Miami's oldest high-rises, as well the city's largest selection of Marcasite jewelry.

Located close to the eye of the storm, Hurricane Andrew caused about $1 million in damage to Cauley Square, catapulting it once again into dilapidation mode. This was not the Village's first experience with natural disasters, being thoroughly ravaged by the Hurricane of 1926, and it would suffer again with Hurricane Wilma in 2005. The Village reopened in 1994 with a historical designation, but it would be at least another decade before things were back to their original illustrious beauty.

Frances Varela, a Honduran immigrant with experience in the construction industry, purchased Cauley Square in 2001, and she is its latest savior. She has spent millions refurbishing it to its memorable beginnings, incorporating lush landscaping, fountains, and elaborate walkways. The Village is not yet in the clear and still remains in danger of closure due its remote location and the overall fragile economic market. Now, more than ever, it is a must see when visiting the area. As a note of caution, beware of the raccoons meandering about.

CHURCHILL'S PUB

5501 NE SECOND AVE. • MIAMI, FL 33137

(305) 757-1807 • CHURCHILLSPUB.COM

Miami's Sort-of English Pub

A recent documentary that Churchill's Pub produced opens with the following: "Beware. Beyond this door is the sanctum of outcasts of the traditional, shunners of the commonplace, and the embracers of musical deviancy. Enter at your own risk." Mr. C, the pub's longtime doorman, affirms, "I cannot see many of these people [Churchill's patrons] go anywhere else. It is a landmark, that is for sure."

Miami is known for many things, but an English pub and overall British tradition is not one of them. Sure, you will see British tourists here on vacation, but residents are few and far in between. Dave Daniels, Churchill's owner, is probably Miami's most popular Brit. In 1979 he founded the club that "from its grotty interior to its Bowery-esque surroundings—is the CBGB of Miami. Everything happens at Churchill's," said musician Rachel Goodrich in a November 28, 2008 *New York Times* article, "South Florida, Tropical Bohemia in the Makings." "It is so real. It is old and it is magical, and there are a lot of secrets there."

Located in the heart of Little Haiti, this little piece of England is juxtaposition incarnate. Daniels named the pub after Winston Churchill because he was an important part of every Brit's life growing up. The white cement establishment looks like an old pub in England, and Churchill's face looms overhead as you walk in. The front room features billiard tables; there is the Laundry Room in the back, the tented patio, and, finally, the main room with the stage. Fair warning: The bathrooms are disgusting. Churchill's was also the first in the city to install dozens of satellites for soccer games; it is World Cup

central. Back in the day, they used to serve bangers and mash, York-shire pudding, and fish and chips.

Daniels notes that pubs in England are the social fabric of a town, and he wanted to bring that experience to Miami. "I have always been into live music. I opened my first jazz club [in England] in 1960," he says. Dating back to 1948, Churchill's Pub was originally C&H Pub, a neighborhood beer and wine bar that closed at 7 p.m.

Three years in, Daniels expanded the hole-in-the-wall and began incorporating live music. At this point, it is circa 1982 and Flynn's Ocean 71 in Miami Beach had just closed down. The so-called scene, which encompasses underground music mostly of the alternative and punk genres, consisted of about a hundred people at the time, and they now had nowhere to go. Daniels gave them a chance, and that is how it all started. Without him, a lot of bands would not have flour-ished. For a long time, Churchill's was the only place to play. It is not just indie or rock, it just *is*. No city has anything like this. Anyone can play onstage. Even the author of this book has taken the stage with a drag queen.

According to "South Florida, Tropical Bohemia in the Makings," "For bands, the city's physical isolation presents obstacles. Whereas musicians in the Northeast can tour from one major city to another to build a regional fan base, for Miamians it's about an 11-hour drive to Atlanta, the next musical mecca. 'Geographically it's a struggle to get out of South Florida,' Mr. Jeffries said.

"And the transient nature of a city full of tourists and immigrants fosters a nightlife that's built around partying. The music that D.J.s spin in local clubs is heavily beat driven: hip-hop, techno, trance. Until recently, the primary outlet for the alternative crowd was the experimental electronic genre called intelligent dance music. Fortunately for Miami rock fans there is Churchill's."

Churchill's Pub is the home of the International Noise Conference, launched in 2003 by Rat Bastard, who you can find on a bar chair most every night of the week. The conference is not for the faint of heart; there is a lot of screaming, howling, vomiting, and blood. Bands like Assholeparade, The Casualties, Agnostic Front, The Vibrators, Slapshot, The Slackers, Raffa and Rainier, Buddy Miles, Lemuria, and Jacuzzi Boys have all played at Churchill's, and even Marilyn Manson reportedly got their start there. This shows the variety of the establishment's live music. You will be able to find everything from hillbilly to burlesque to ambient doom, mellow acoustic, and blues alternative.

"He [Daniels] has always been good to people. He gives people a chance, as long as they bring a crowd and drinking," says longtime bartender Nicky Bowe. In the eighties, the wife of a frequent customer set up a tailor station in the middle of the bar, offering her services. To add some nostalgia to everyone's lives, Nicky's wife brought it back for a week.

Local writer and Churchill's Pub patron and expert Liz Tracy has provided Miami with frequent updates on the happenings of the pub. "My experience at Churchill's is fairly typical. I began coming here at sixteen and loved it from the beginning. I guess I am attracted to gross shit. They used to have a theater underground where I used to read poetry in the back of the pub. Back in the day, it was popular to go to Fox's for dinner with your parents, then stay at the bar, then go to Churchill's. And then when Churchill's closed, it was off to Mac's Club Deuce on the beach."

"For decades, Monday night was jazz night," Tracy continues. "Like everyone knows bands started here. Churchill's is an incubator for music. They were known for letting bands have an audience to experiment and test material such as noise music, Dick Dale, and all

the big bands. Some people may even play by themselves, doesn't matter if the music sucks. The strangest and probably scariest performance I saw was by Costes, a French performer, who liked to shock his audience with feces and other inappropriate items. More than anything, it was disgusting.

Closing rumors have been around for years, but sadly Churchill's Pub was finally sold in the earlier part of 2014; at seventy-four years old, Daniels is ready to move on. He is old and tired; he just does not want to do it anymore. "Me, I love it so much that I want to be buried here."

At the time of this writing, the pub was sold, but what changes may come are still unknown. It is an institution and the buyers, who are anonymous at the moment, say they want to keep the establishment the same.

THE CLAY HOTEL

1438 WASHINGTON AVE. • MIAMI BEACH, FL 33139

(305) 534-2988 • CLAYHOTEL.COM

Miami Beach's Enchanting Hotel

A Mediterranean palace on Española Way, the Clay Hotel's motto can be felt from the moment one walks through its breezy doors: A unique blend of superb location, unbeatable value, and enchanting atmosphere.

Unlike many hotels in Miami Beach, this one is not located oceanfront, but two blocks away on Española Way. The Clay offers a different but welcome side of the area to visitors, an off-the-beaten-path experience. Cecilia Curuthers, the hotel's general manager, who has been at the hotel for sixteen years, explains that the Clay is a time capsule of Miami Beach history. From Al Capone's gambling syndicate, which operated on the hotel's top floors, to Desi Arnaz's rumba days, and serving as the backdrop to shows like *Miami Vice* and music videos such as Ricky Martin's "Non Siamo Soli," the hotel has a very colorful and storied past, much like the street on which it resides.

Located between Washington and Drexel Avenues, Española Way is a half-block pedestrian wonderland featuring open-air markets, live music and entertainment, and restaurants. Brought to life in the early twenties, N.T.B. Roney created the village to fulfill his dream of a Mediterranean-style bohemian community for artists and writers, where the background served as inspiration. Once known as the Old Spanish Village, Española Way was an instant sensation. On April 11, 1926, the *Miami News* radiated the enthusiasm with the headline: "Roney's Spanish Village has atmosphere and charm of Castile."

The same Roney who simultaneously commissioned the illustrious Roney Palace on another stretch of the island built the Clay Hotel in

1925. The hotel's architecture is Mediterranean with a twenties Florida style, including a wooden arched entryway, small wrought-iron balconies, a tiled roof, winding passageways, a peach-colored exterior with red-and-white awnings, and a front desk that has been the same since 1925. Each window features a different shape, and decorative flamingos welcome guests. It was not always nice, though; there was a heavy anti-Semitic movement during Miami Beach's boom years, and renovations in the 2000s unearthed a large sign on one of the hotel's walls that reads Gentiles Only.

While the rest of the city flourished, Española Way's popularity decreased between the decades of the forties and eighties, due to the rising danger of Al Capone's gambling ring, military occupation of the area, racism, and overall dilapidation of buildings. Its balmy weather and flat lands made Miami a popular area for army and navy training base camps. Hailing from all reaches of the country, military personnel called many of the city's hotels home during World War II. At the conclusion of the war, many soldiers decided to make Miami their permanent residence, though most GIs evacuated the hotels by the end of 1945. Changing demographics in the sixties and seventies brought even more grittiness to the area. The all-night parties and dancing in the streets had been permanently replaced by bums in the streets and dilapidated buildings.

In 1979 Linda Polansky brought fresh thinking and renewed hope to the area. A former banker, she got into the real estate game locally. She did not sell condos or rent high-rise apartments; instead, she looked for buyers for old, rundown hotels and apartment houses—in this case, most of the Art Deco buildings of Miami Beach. One such buyer was Barbara Capitman, who is credited with changing much of the face of South Beach with her preservation dreams and sparking the Art Deco preservation movement. The eighties proved to be a tumultuous decade in Miami, and the Clay Hotel, located in the heart of the action, experienced many changes, growing pains, and important events during this time.

First was the change in lodging category from hotel to hostel and then came the introduction of the peach color to the hotel's exterior. Polansky was interested in reviving the neighborhood with brighter colors, moving away from the drab creams and browns. In stepped Mel Bourne, a production designer for the popular show *Miami Vice*, who shared an interest in Española Way and the color peach. Armed

with a new paint job, the hotel played background in many of the show's episodes.

The Clay also served as the base for a controversial crime-fighting group called the Guardian Angels. They set up shop in a storefront donated by the hotel. They chose to open a Miami chapter because of the high crime rate against the city's elderly. At the same time, there was an overpopulation problem with the Cuban refugees from the Mariel boatlifts. These refugees were initially given hospice at Miami hotels to be paid for by the government, until the government breached the contract. At one point, thirty refugees called the Clay Hotel home. The city was littered with crime, which kept many of the locals indoors and scared and tourists away.

"Española Way has grown up a lot, and most recently, it has finally come into its own," says hotel manager Curuthers. "Like a teenager going through puberty, there were some awkward years in between. In the 2009–10 season, we made the big decision to convert the hostel back to a hotel with 138 rooms. It was a big change, but one that was needed." These days, the charismatic street abounds with tourists and locals alike. Española Way still retains its bohemian charm with boutique shops and restaurants, and offers a welcome respite from the nearby bustling streets.

COLONY THEATRE

1040 LINCOLN RD. • MIAMI BEACH, FL 33139

(305) 674-1040 • COLONYTHEATREMIAMIBEACH.COM

The Beauty Queen

Known to many as Miami's "Beauty Queen," Paramount Pictures opened the Colony Theatre as a movie house in 1935. Originally seating 1,200 individuals, the theater opened to great fanfare. On opening night, eccentric bombshell Carole Lombard made a special appearance for the inaugural program of *Clive of India*. Some of the most popular films to grace the screen include *Alfie*, *The Sound of Music*, *Doctor Zhivago*, and *The Great Race*.

The Colony is located on majestic Lincoln Road in Miami Beach, an outdoor pedestrian mall that spans seven blocks and is nestled between Washington Avenue and Alton Road, featuring bright yellow awnings, outdoor tables and seating, and bright colors on the sidewalks against the backdrop of stores and restaurants. Lincoln Road has experienced many ups, downs, expansions, and renovations, and the theater's business is directly influenced by the mall's success or lack thereof. The Colony has functioned as both a movie theater and a live performance theater and has gone back and forth between the two for what was needed at the time.

The dream of Carl Fisher, one of Miami Beach's foremost developers, Lincoln Road was designed to be the Fifth Avenue of the South, and in its heyday included such prominent retailers as Saks Fifth Avenue, Bonwit Teller, and Elizabeth Arden. For relaxation and noshing before a screening, it was popular to visit The Noshery at the Saxon Hotel. During that time the mall's popularity boomed, and tourists and residents alike were enthralled. It was normal to see visitors dressed in their finest threads, women clad in white gloves and

jewels, while men donned their best top hats and ties. A nostalgic article in the *News-Journal* on October 5, 1988, recalled those glory days: "In the 1940s and 1950s, when this resort town was the country's foremost vacation spot, Lincoln Road was the commercial and social center of Miami Beach." The Colony Theatre was located in the heart of the action.

In the fifties the theater was converted into a performing arts venue. In the sixties Morris Lapidus remodeled Lincoln Road in the MiMo style. During that same decade the theater was converted back into a movie house. While Miami was not known for its arts until the later 2000s, an initiative from 1971 shows its underground progressiveness. The *Miami News* reported that the theater was purchased by Samuel Kipnis to house the Greater Miami Educational Cultural Series, a nonprofit subscription organization. He supplied films from his private library of 500 titles. Subscription cards were $50 each and good for fifty-two admissions.

In the eighties the Colony was converted back to a live performance theater, as it remains today. The biggest news of the decade came from the Miami City Ballet announcing the theater as its permanent home. The Miami City Ballet came in at an interesting time; the mall was undergoing a large artist revolution that included the opening of two other famous spots, Books & Books and Wet Paint Cafe. To accommodate the new residents, the Colony retrofitted its front windows so that passersby could watch the ballet dancers during practice.

The nineties was a tough decade for Miami overall, and the mall saw a heavy decline and general dilapidation, unlike any of decades past. On July 15, 1994, the *Boca Raton News* reported on a small production by Acme Acting Company titled *Jeffrey*, a romantic comedy about gay lovers, relationships, and AIDS. Even with a taboo subject (at the time), a record high of 800 people filled the theater.

Most recently the mall and the theater have seen a fruitful revival. In 2006 a major $6.5 million renovation returned the Colony to its illustrious 1935 glory, with a focus on the original facade in the Art Deco style. The renovation also included the addition of lighting, rigging, and a professional sound system. The theater is now owned by the City of Miami Beach, and after its many renovations throughout the decades, it has been downsized to an intimate venue of 415 stadium-style seats, guaranteeing a spectacular and clear view from each and every seat in the house.

Another reason why the Colony Theatre has survived decades is because of its diverse lineup. As a rental theater, all productions are limited-engagement events and range from opera, ballet, orchestras, and plays to flamenco, burlesque, comedy shows, and modern concerts.

Marione Van Steensburg has worked at the theater for eighteen years. Some of her favorite performances came courtesy of the Miami Lyric Opera. She notes that one of the Colony's most notable productions was *Cleopatra*, in association with the Royal Shakespeare Company. "The Royal Shakespeare Company is a big deal! For them to use us as a venue was a great experience. Another great tidbit, many people do not know that the Colony Theatre was styled for both the performer and the listener. Having been in the industry for decades, this is a small but crucial detail that really sets us apart and that many overlook."

On a final note, the theater is reportedly haunted. The Miami Para-normal Research Society has recorded and reported various paranor-mal sightings at the property, the bulk of these incidents taking place behind the main stage. "Great names have graced the stage, many claiming the theater as their beloved second home, and while haunt-ings and apparitions are a possibility, I think it is mostly bologna," says Van Steensburg.

The Colony Theatre is listed on the National Register of Historic Places. Another landmark from the same era, the Lincoln Theatre, was recently gutted and restructured for a large retail store. Built in 1936 in the Art Deco style, the theater was the previous home of the New World Symphony and stood alongside the Colony as a reminder of old-world style. Fortunately, the Colony Theatre remains as a bea-con for the importance and continuity of all art forms in the city.

COOPERTOWN RESTAURANT

22700 SW EIGHTH ST. • MIAMI, FL 33194

(305) 226-6048

Catfish and Frog Legs and Gator Tail, Oh My!

Since the early nineties, Miami's suburban revolution has steadily crept into the heart of the Everglades, and it is a surprise that Coopertown Restaurant is still in existence. This chapter arguably offers the most important story in the book, as it is more than just the story of a small restaurant preserving traditional Florida fare. There is a deeper message, the one revealing the slow demise of one of the country's most important natural treasures, the Everglades.

Coopertown has been selling traditional Florida fare of catfish, frog legs, and gator tail since 1967. It may not be the only place you can get gator and frog legs in Miami, but it is the most exciting and the most unique. In terms of food, the main draw remains the delectable frog legs. The restaurant is so iconic that it was recently included in the quirky book by locals Roxanne Vargas and Maruchi Mendez, *100 Things to Do in Miami Before You Die*.

Located in the far reaches of Miami and on the border of the Everglades, getting there is equally an adventure. Driving out to Coopertown can be a little daunting the first time around. At Krome Avenue the road becomes two lanes, and only miles of swamp and vegetation are visible. The only barrier between you and nature is the car. This road is more traditionally known as Tamiami Trail, and in vast contrast to Alligator Alley or I-75, it offers no barriers from the wildlife.

In under an hour, you are instantly transported to a different world. Soon the billboards appear: airboat rides, Indian villages, wildlife exhibits, and Coopertown. Once you arrive, there is a trio of shacks

COOPERTOWN
RESTAURANT

MENU

FROGLEGS
ALLIGATOR TAIL

ALSO...

BREAKFAST
SANDWICHES

EXPRESSO, SODA & BEER

AND MUCH MORE!

SHIRT-SHOES REQUIRED
NO PETS ALLOWED

with distinct purposes: The main shack in the center houses the restaurant, the second houses a resting area and is the starting point for the airboat rides, and the third is a bait shop. The white restaurant is small, seating only about twenty people. Old Florida nostalgia hits you with the assortment of souvenirs for sale. Business cards from years of visitors and customers cover the ceiling. Gator skulls are the decor of choice, but that is part of the charm.

One of the most unique things about Coopertown Restaurant is that it is located in Coopertown, an unincorporated town within the confines of Miami-Dade County that has a population of eight people. Yes, you read that correctly, eight people. There is even a mayor. John Cooper, a non-Florida native from Chicago, seeking the great South Florida dream, founded it in 1945. It is now owned and operated by the Kennon family, descendants of the Coopers.

The Kennons came from Missouri, where they had their own frogging business, lured by grand tales of exceptional Everglades frogging. The town's seven airboats, which now serve as the main draw, were originally used for frogging, but as the tourists came and showed interest, their use changed. Coopertown is the oldest airboat tour operator on this side of the Everglades. The restaurant and town's success is directly influenced by the traffic on the Tamiami Trail; luckily it is heavily used, as it serves as the main thoroughfare between Miami and the west side of Florida to cities like Naples and Sanibel.

The most important regional and indigenous Miami foods are those that are available in the Everglades. Move over foie gras, alligator and frogs are our area's delicacies. But even so, the trade of frogging has been in a steady decline since the eighties, another reason for the

Vintage Spot
MACK'S FISH CAMP: EST. 1944

Airboat rides, alligators, and fishing. Get in touch with the beauty of the Everglades with the last of a dying breed, the Gladesman.

Danell Lane; (954) 536-7400; macksfishcamp.com

demise of overall airboat usage. Even then, frog hunting was rare. This is in sharp contrast to the early 1900s, when Florida was the frog capital of the country. Tallahassee's *News-Journal* quoted a local on September 15, 1988, stating that no one can really make a living catching frogs anymore. Most of the frog legs consumed in the United States are imported. Today, Coopertown Restaurant sources their frog meat from Central Florida, receiving upwards of a hundred pounds a month.

The original Gladesmen hunt frogs in the traditional way, but as it is a dying business, there are only an estimated ten to twelve of them doing it on a full-time basis. These Gladesmen are the last of a dying breed. They are the men who grew up in the Everglades and live off of the land, who know the culture and landscape of this vast land like no other, built upon generation after generation of oral tradition. In modern times, their formerly isolated lives and role in society are changing as well.

If you are interested in frogging, there are still ways to seek it out in the Everglades. February and March are peak season, mainly because the water levels are low enough for the frogs to come to the top and feed. Coopertown takes visitors on special trips upon request, but know that frogging's best hours are between four and six in the morning. If you would rather forgo sleep deprivation and eat them already prepared, the must-try dish is the Everglades Combination Dinner consisting of six frog legs, a third of a pound of gator, french fries, coleslaw, and garlic bread.

DONUT GALLERY DINER

83 HARBOR DR. • KEY BISCAYNE, FL 33149

(305) 361-9985 • DONUTGALLERYDINER.COM

A Key Biscayne Tradition

William John Matheson, one of Miami's pioneers, moved to the South Florida area in the early 1900s. Many recognize his name from the popular beach park in South Dade, Matheson Hammocks Park, but few know that he was one of the main catalysts for the island of Key Biscayne. He used part of the island for the development of a coconut plantation and experimental fruit groves. The island remained isolated until November 1947, when the Rickenbacker Causeway was constructed.

Outside of Miami, Key Biscayne is best known for being Richard Nixon's playground. It remains an interesting place that serves many purposes: an off-the-beaten-path destination for tourists, a tennis haven for locals, and an overall residential community that is serene and where life remains slow and tropical-like and the speed limit remains at 20 miles per hour.

"The only landmarks left around here are Oasis Sandwich Shop and Mangrove Cycles," says Donut Gallery Diner owner Ota Zambrano. "And when I say landmarks, I mean places that have been around for more than twenty years. Can you believe Chief's Sushi and Seafood Market closed two months ago? A lot of places are shutting down due to changing demographics and higher rents. The local demographics used to be made up primarily of snowbirds; these days there's a larger influx of Latin Americans. It is definitely a different but welcome change that adds more spice to the local flavor, pun intended. The current population of Key Biscayne includes celebrities and wealthy Colombians, Venezuelans, Peruvians, and Brazilians."

According to local and regular Marianne Pantin, "Although the name reads Donut Gallery Diner, the least requested item may be the donuts. Regulars, which include old Key Rats [the common name for residents of Key Biscayne] who have eaten there for twenty to thirty years, stop by from early to mid-afternoon to have their coffee and read the *Miami Herald*—watch out Starbucks."

A local favorite since 1972, Donut Gallery is an institution on Key Biscayne, and there is usually a line out the door. It is one of the oldest establishments on the island and a simple place. Even more rare, they are open every single day of the year and only close early on the Fourth of July, Thanksgiving, and Christmas.

Originally from Cuba, Benjamin Zambrano, father of owner Nelson Zambrano, moved to New York in 1948. Much as it is today, Miami and New York were strongly interlaced cities, and he heard about the available donut shop through the grapevine. He picked up his family and moved to Key Biscayne. The Donut Gallery became the Donut Gallery Diner, a breakfast and lunch diner. From day one, Zambrano opened at 5:30 a.m. "Police on an early shift, truck drivers passing through, and fishermen who needed a good start to the day were all appreciative of the early opening time," says Pantin. "Now you will easily find lounging grandmothers, soccer moms and kids before games, executives, and beachgoers sitting shoulder to shoulder at the counter."

The best owners are the ones that were customers first. Ota was a regular at the diner prior to meeting her husband, Nelson Zambrano. Her favorite item on the menu, along with many others, is the TED Special. "'A TED, please,' or 'A TED's Double' is all you need to say," Pantin explains. "This has been a staple for as long as I can remember, and there is nothing low-cal, farm-to-table, or gastro about this. An open-faced English muffin with eggs, bacon, ham, cheese, and tomatoes starts your day, so you don't worry about hunger pangs until the late afternoon." The famous TED Special was created for customers of the now-defunct Stefano's nightclub, offering a great remedy to a long night of dancing and debauchery.

The owners' lives center around the community of Key Biscayne, and they love it. Nelson and Ota got married at the Cape Florida Light, another historic landmark on the island. The restaurant's walls further illustrate this, as they are lined with great memories of the

Key, both old and new. With the rise of technology, pictures can be seen on the video screens above the counter, too.

Donut Galley Diner is a diner through and through, but there is no coleslaw or pickles or potato salad. They serve breakfast and lunch all day, and favorites include BLTs, burgers, chili dogs, eggs, and pancakes. The twenty-four-seat diner features a Formica-countertop bar with vinyl stools and a handful of side tables along with a bois-terous environment, creating a nostalgic experience. In the days of Benjamin Zambrano, the diner closed at 1:30 p.m., but when Nelson took over, they extended their hours to 3 p.m. Interestingly enough, the diner also remains a popular spot post-hurricane, serving as a hub for information, food, and community.

The restaurant is a family team, too. "Uncle Raul works the regis-ter. Laurie has been here for thirty years. Ruth on the prep station has been around for twenty years, and our cook Ana has been around for ten years," says Zambrano. "At the Donut Gallery," Pantin adds, "you are never alone since Laurie, a thirty-plus-year employee, remembers your name, your kids' names, and your parents' names, who, by the way, will probably be up on the picture wall, a source of pride should you be given that status." Pantin concludes, "Tourists, who come time and again to visit Key Biscayne [people we actually know], would not leave without a stop at the Donut Gallery. It might be a hole-in-the-wall in a strip mall, but it fills a large part of Key Biscayne's history and a big space in Key Biscayners' hearts and memory books."

EL REY DE LAS FRITAS

1821 SW EIGHTH ST. • MIAMI, FL 33135

(305) 644-6054 • ELREYDELASFRITAS.COM

Frita: The Cuban Hamburger

The *frita* is more Cuban than a Cuban sandwich. It is the food you do not tell the non-Cubans about for fear of exploitation," says JC Lopez in a 2011 *Edible South Florida* article.

We do everything differently in Miami, including the burgers. In Miami, burgers are *fritas*. Of Cuban descent, the burger is made up of ground beef seasoned with paprika and other spices, cooked on a flattop, and topped with onions and julienne potatoes on a Cuban roll. Priced at $3.25, they are a steal. There are many restaurants, even non-Cuban ones, that make and sell the fast-food staple, but only one holds the crown—El Rey de las Fritas. It is so popular that it has been visited by the likes of Rachael Ray, Anthony Bourdain, Bobby Flay, and George Motz, America's hamburger expert.

But, the battle of the *frita* in Miami has a long history, and holding the crown has been no easy feat. El Rey's biggest competitor is El Mago de las Fritas, which has its own Rolodex of famous visitors, including President Barack Obama. Around Miami, there is a great *frita* divide, and die-hard fans take it as seriously as soccer fanatics do *futbol*.

El Rey de las Fritas is a family empire. Opened by Victoriano Gonzalez, it is now owned and operated by daughter Mercedes "Mercy" Gonzalez. Papa Gonzalez opened the original *frita* stand with his brothers at the young age of thirteen in his hometown of Placetas on the porch of a pharmacy in the town square. To orient you with the geography of Cuba, Placetas is located in the middle of the country. All pueblos, or villages, had a *frita* stand, which are most related to

the hot dog stands of today. After the Cuban Revolution, Victoriano took the long route to Miami, living in Spain and New Jersey before setting up shop.

"When they first arrived to Miami, my mom worked at the Holiday Inn in Miami Beach and my dad worked at a shrimp factory for eight to nine years," says Mercy. "He saved his money and opened his first restaurant." Ortelio Cardenas, Gonzalez's brother-in-law, learned how to make *fritas* at El Rey. After a fallout, he went on to open his own restaurant, El Mago de las Fritas, but this is not a story about El Mago.

Fritas came to Miami with a long Cuban history. Miami is an extension of Cuba, and like many other stories in this book, Cuba's *frita* pioneers had to relocate their successful businesses across the Caribbean. *Fritas* most likely originated in the thirties; the exact date is unclear, but it ranges between the thirties and fifties, depending on whom you ask. *El rey*, or the king, Victoriano Gonzalez, was not the first to introduce the *frita* to Miami. Ramon Estevill is the pioneer who brought the delicacy to the city in 1962 and opened his fourteen-seat restaurant Fritas Domino on Calle Ocho (Eighth Street) and 12th Avenue.

The original Fritas Domino is long gone, but El Rey de las Fritas opened in its place. The location eventually burned down, and El Rey moved to its current location in 2008. To make things even more confusing, before it was El Rey, it originally opened as El Palacio de las Fritas, aka the Palace of the Fritas, in the seventies on Eighth Street and 67th Avenue. The location on Eighth Street was the first and the longest running. Now, there is a location in Hialeah, which is operated by Mercy's mother, and a location in Westchester, which is operated by Mercy's brother.

In the new generation, Mercy just wants to continue the legacy her hardworking father created and honor him. She grew up in the restaurant; those who have frequented the restaurant for years may remember a young Mercy in the back office doing homework or twirling in her chair, or even behind the counter selling burgers.

"It is no longer about what nightclub you went to, but what food you ate, and we have to keep up with the trends," Mercy says. "Like cigars and wine, the entire food industry is trend-driven, but to go with the cliché, we, as a restaurant, have only gotten better with time. To keep up with the changing trends, we have incorporated a food truck; added the option of adding cheese to the *frita*, which used to be a sin; and, finally, one of our newest additions includes a *frita* topped with sweet plantains.

"Each restaurant varies a bit. The Westchester location is simple and offers the original menu. The Hialeah and Calle Ocho menus have more Cuban products. My mother makes all food from scratch every morning, and the Friday specials like *rabo encendido* [oxtail stew] are the best. *Pan con butifarra*, which is a sausage sandwich, is one of the few I have seen on menus across town. My father always wanted to make a fast-food and to-go restaurant. I have seen it all; we are popular with tourists and locals alike, but the old customers are the best. They are usually older and have come around for so long that they feel like they have the authority to call us out if our food is off. It keeps us on our toes."

Cigar Titans

The small store is located on iconic Calle Ocho in Little Havana. From the second you walk in, you realize that it is not like any other cigar store around. The spicy and sweet scent of tobacco immediately hits your nostrils, and the lively Spanish music in the background transports you to another world. A total of six long wooden tables serve as the workstations for nine Master Rollers who work all day to produce the impeccable product that is the hand-packed and -rolled cigar. For those who want only a small taste of the cigars, you can buy mini cigarillos from the jar that reads "Smuggled Cuban cigars; stolen from Castro's private stash." A jovial nod to the old country and the hope, shared by many, to one day return.

Even if you do not like cigars, you can always appreciate a good history. The store is named after Antonio Maceo, also known as El Titan de Bronze, a big mulatto who fought on horseback clad in the color bronze. The brand and cigar labels feature a shield and a machete, items Maceo always had with him. He was a hero of the Cuban War of Independence and died fighting the Spaniards. At nearby Cuban Memorial Plaza, a bust of Maceo stands.

The factory makes four different styles of cigars: Titan de Bronze Gold, Titan Grand Reserve Maduro, Titan Grand Reserve Cameroon, and Titan Redemption Sun Grown Habano. They create their own secret mix from a variety of leaves from the Dominican Republic, Nicaragua, Honduras, North America, Indonesia, and Brazil. A lot goes into tobacco production and, unfortunately, the store is too small to

age or ferment tobacco leaves themselves. Boxes of cigars range in price from $80 to $140 and individually as low as $4.

Established in 1995 by Don Carlos Covin, El Titan is now run by his daughter Sandy, who immediately notes that the tobacco game is becoming more and more of a woman's world. "Tobacco industries are generally family owned and operated. This industry is all I have known my entire life, and I absolutely love it. My uncle made custom art for cigar boxes, and that is how my dad got into the business—the beauty got him."

Back when El Titan opened in the nineties, Little Havana was not safe and tourists were few and far between. "Now, we get everyone in here, French, Swedish, Asian—you name it," Sandy says. "Germans are our biggest clients; they smoke a lot of cigars" In the sixties the area was a manufacturing hub for cigars, but all the big manufacturers such as Padron and Oliva are long gone. Much like the sixties, Little Havana is returning to its roots and becoming a haven for tobacco lovers, with at least a dozen cigar stores for the choosing and another half-dozen cigar manufacturers.

Nine Level 9 rollers, who have worked in world-renowned factories such as Romeo y Julieta and Partagas, handcraft all of the store's cigars. At the end of the day, another Master Roller and/or Blender inspect each day's work. All of El Titan's rollers are hired through personal recommendation and are generally the crème de la crème. Sandy says that each roller makes between eighty and one hundred cigars each day.

Cigars are similar to wine, and selection of the seeds, terroir, and tasting are all extremely important. Cigar rolling began in Cuba and then expanded to the Dominican Republic and Nicaragua, in that order. Sandy notes that Dominican cigars are more mellow and sweet, while Nicaraguan cigars are stronger and spicy, but nothing beats a Cuban. In traditional cigar culture, Cuba is known as the Holy Grail, producing the best cigars in the world. Because of political instability and general isolation, the art of Cuban cigar rolling is being preserved in other parts of the world. The traditional Cuban method of rolling is done with single workers, while most other countries do it in teams. El Titan employs this traditional form of Cuban rolling.

Females did not roll cigars until the introduction of El Laguito in the sixties. As one of the world's most famous cigar factories, it is housed in a palatial old mansion in an upscale suburb of Havana, and it is where the first Cohiba was rolled. Celia Sánchez Manduley, Fidel Castro's Secretary to the Presidency of the Council of Ministers and Major Participant of the Revolution, was the leader of the renowned training program. Maria Sierra, El Titan's top roller, is a 95 rated, Level 9 roller and spent thirty years at El Laguito. Sanchez Manduley hired young ladies between the ages of seventeen and eighteen. Hundreds of girls applied, and Sierra was able to get a position. To be invited to work at El Laguito is a privilege. They have a distinct way of making cigar tips into a fan.

In honor of Samuel Paley, the factory has exclusively begun producing limited-edition La Palina cigars called La Palina Collection Goldie and La Palina Collection Mr. Sam. Master Roller Maria Sierra, who signs each numbered box, rolls the entire La Palina Collection Goldie. Named for the wife of Sam Paley, Goldie Drell Paley, it celebrates women in the cigar industry. If you recognize the Paley name, it is because William "Bill" Paley, son of Sam and Goldie, was the founder of CBS. Many do not know that the company has roots in the cigar world. As a Ukrainian immigrant, his first job in the United States was lector for a cigar factory. These days, most workers in cigar factories gossip and listen to music on their iPods.

FIFTEENTH STREET BOOKS

296 ARAGON AVE. • CORAL GABLES, FL 33134

(305) 442-2344

That Other Bookstore on Aragon

Fifteenth Street Books is indeed that other bookstore on Aragon Avenue, located only a few doors and steps away from the famed Books & Books. Both are completely different, and both are equally worth a visit.

Located just one block from Miracle Mile, it is easy to walk past the unassuming store. The exterior is equally exquisite once you know it is there. The store's front doors are bordered with a Roman-style design, both regal and classic. Its windows are lined with books enticing customers to go in as they walk past. Once inside, the smell of old books hits you immediately. It is a magical gem for lovers of all things old, and it's truly difficult not to fall in love. The dark and cozy store features an interesting setup that includes curios, wooden shelves, and rolling ladders that resembles a grandparent's home, if their home was a bookstore.

One thing to remember is that this is not the type of place where you walk in with a specific item in mind, but plan to immerse yourself in the space and spend hours perusing one-of-a-kind treasures. Fifteenth Street Books is actually three stores in one and sells books, antiques, armoires, jewelry, purses, mirrors, exquisite chairs, old music sheets, trinkets and tchotchkes, fine art, china, tea sets, maps, and lamps.

Perusing the store, I stumbled upon some unique titles like Plato's *Theaetetus, Sophist and Statesman, Vienna and Its Jews: The Tragedy of Success 1880s–1980s, The Poems of Robert Burns, A Ring of Bells,* Eavan Boland's books, *The Diary of an Ad Man, The Law and*

the Word, *Epochs of Chinese and Japanese Art*, *France the Beautiful Cookbook*, *Gardiner's Cruising North America*, *Peru Before Pizarro*, *Salud!: A South American Journal*, *The Camellia*, *Jardins de la Cote d'Azur*, *Birds of America*, *The Frederic Remington Art Museum Collection*, *Art Treasures of the Hermitage*, *The Art Institute of Chicago: 100 Masterpieces*, *Raining Sardines*, *El Conde de Cuchicute*, and autographed Ernest Hemingway novels. For Florida enthusiasts, there is an entire section on the state's history with a special emphasis on South Florida.

While this is a quaint store, there is a backstory buried behind its walls. The store's distinguished owner, Julius Ser, is Mitchell Kaplan's (owner of Books & Books) uncle and former partner. Ser and Kaplan opened the original Books & Books at the location of Fifteenth Street Books in 1982. Prior to Books & Books, the site housed a watch repair shop. Books & Books was a hit from the first day it opened, but the partnership between Ser and Kaplan dissolved in 1998 after claims that Ser held back profits from Kaplan, among other allegations. The present incarnation of Fifteenth Street Books opened in 2001. From

Vintage Spot
DUNBAR OLD BOOKS: 2000

Step into a maze of used and out-of-print books, antiques, and one-of-a-kind finds. Dunbar specializes in the topics of religion, science, and history. It is easy to spend hours perusing their rare collection of over 15,000 books.

7061 SW 46th St.; (305) 669-8719; dunbarbooks.com

a young age, Ser was a lover of books, especially antiquarian books. He is a Miamian, a graduate of Miami Beach High School and longtime resident of Coral Gables.

The inventory at Fifteenth Street Books changes on an almost daily basis, and Ser loves to buy items from regulars who bring in their wares. While they specialize in art dealing, Latin American products, and first editions, Ser purchases whatever tickles his brain and has no real guidelines. Prices are fair and range from as little as $3 to as high as hundreds of dollars, naturally depending on the item.

Independent bookstores are instrumental to communities, providing literary life, and this is one to visit and appreciate before it disappears like many other unique bookstores, such as La Moderna Poesia, West Kendall Bookshelf, and Downtown Book Center. But while bookstores all over the country are on a steady decline, fret not. Nathaniel Sandler quoted P. Scott Cunningham on WLRN about the state of Miami's own literary culture: "Literary culture is healthy, alive, and well in South Florida. We have always had a good community and will continue to work at it." One thing is for sure—there is no other place like this in Miami.

FOOTBALL SANDWICH SHOP

8484 NW SECOND AVE. • MIAMI, FL 33138
(305) 759-3602 • FOOTBALLSANDWICHSHOP.COM

Home of the Zonker

Football Sandwich Shop is a great lesson for those who like to judge books by their cover. The lesson: Do not do it! Housed in a Pepto-Bismol-colored converted gas station with barred windows, it does not look inviting, appetizing, or even remotely like a place that would serve fresh, high-quality sub sandwiches. The shop's signs, visible from far distances, note otherwise, of course.

Miamians love to complain, and the lack of good sandwich shops is just another item on the list. Other than the cult following of Publix subs, Miami is not really known as a sub town, like our friends to the north. While the proper history of the sub sandwich is unknown, it is said to have originated in Italian-American communities in the Northeast and named "submarine" or "sub" because it resembles the ship of the same name.

"I have lived in Miami Shores forever and it really is a landmark, an institution," says Football Sandwich Shop regular Ines Hegedus-Garcia. "The owner Doug even recognizes my voice when I call in to place an order. It is just simple and quick good food and the type of place you do not find anymore."

Located on the fringes of El Portal on Miami's Little River, Richard Hage opened the shop in 1973 after he noticed that Miami lacked an overall sub culture or even a good place to get sandwiches. Football Sandwich Shop is his ode to the New York–style sub and to something even more interesting. When Hage opened the restaurant, people were absolutely Miami Dolphins crazy, with capital letters. Led by Coach Don Shula and players Bob Griese, Earl Morrall, and Larry

Csonka, the Dophins had just played the NFL's first perfect season. This perfect season led to the inspiration behind the shop's quirky design. And while he was not part of that omnipotent 1972 season, another major theme at the restaurant is Dan Marino, whose name and persona is also synonymous with the Dolphins. Hage now operates the shop along with his son-in-law Doug Estes and it is a family operation, with the rest of the clan helping out in the summer or in their off-time.

Ordering by the number is mandatory, and since I am no football expert, an article from 2005 in the *Miami Herald* describes it best: "The menu features names and jersey numbers that should be familiar to longtime Dolphins fans aka Dolfans. The Zonker, No. 39 on the menu, named after Hall of Fame fullback Larry Csonka, is stuffed with ham, salami and provolone; the egg-salad sub Marv-o-lus, No. 80, is named for former tight end Marv Fleming; and The Best, a turkey and roast beef combo, dedicated to former safety Dick Anderson." At $4.79, the Zonker remains a steal.

Like fellow book entry Mainzer's German Deli, they make their own salads in-house. Everything is homemade, from the salads to the sweet items, including carrot cake, banana nut cake, and chocolate cake, and the famous, huge chocolate chip cookies take you back to childhood. Local chef Michael Gilligan, formerly of Rusty Pelican,

Vintage Spot

SARUSSI SUBS: EST. 1960S

Sarussi offers a twist on the original Cuban sandwich. El Original, or "The Original," comes with sliced ham, roast pork, pickles, and mozzarella and topped with secret sauce. The pièce de résistance, it passes through a pizza oven before finding its way to your plate. Most recently, Sarussi was made famous by Adam Richman of *Man v. Food*, when he tackled their colossal two-and-a-half-pound sandwich.

6797 SW Eighth St.; (305) 264-5464; sarussisubs.com

recommends another classic, the BLT. The sub shop is also a favorite of local law enforcement.

Stepping inside the Football is like taking a trip back in time. For those who want even more of a Miami flashback, there are also several old photos on the walls of the sub shop back when it was a gasoline station. This is one of the most bizarre places you will ever come across, but weirdly enough, it works. Once inside, the trademark Dolphins aqua color, packed tables, and sports memorabilia galore, hanging from the ceiling and plastered all over the walls, greet you. Simply put, it is a sandwich shop that is themed with football memorabilia and a pseudo-shrine to the Miami Dolphins. Over the years, however, it has expanded to include all types of Florida sports memorabilia, even high school sports. An interesting fact, they introduced the concept of fast casual to the Miami area way before the Chipotles of the world showed up around here. Operation-wise, they are still old-school, without a computerized system, and they write orders on scraps of paper. There is even a drive-thru window for those on the go, but still craving a Zonker.

The delicious food and personable service are the main draws here, but if subs are not your thing . . . "go for the breathtakingly amazing Dan Marino lithograph in which there is lightning, dolphins breaking through the sky, and a haircut in the key of David Hasselhoff," says local writer Nathaniel Sandler.

THE FORGE RESTAURANT

432 41ST ST. • MIAMI BEACH, FL 33140

(305) 538-8533 • THEFORGE.COM

A Forge Turned Restaurant

The Forge is like an institution," says local writer Matt Meltzer. "Before every celebrichef in the world decided to open a spot in Miami, it was THE place to be seen. And, like any classic, it is not going to be swayed when competition comes in. Are there steaks just as good on the Beach? You know, probably, but between the over-the-top gothic decor and the wine collection—I took a tour of the expansive space recently, and it is unlike anything I have ever seen—it just still manages to set itself apart.

"Another reason it has persevered is because they are always changing things up. This is especially crucial in Miami, when a new fine-dining spot opens every twenty minutes. As a restaurant, to stay alive and relevant, you always have to be doing something new, and they have done that. I thought former chef Dewey Losasso did some cool stuff with his lobster PB&J and coffee-rubbed steaks; keeping the menu new and whatnot. Their new chef, Christopher Lee, is taking it to the next level. The restaurant still has steak, but now they have this Jamaican jerk bacon with mango, and that is something I have not seen anywhere else. And their new fondue thing is just over the top—dippable Rice Krispies Treats and s'mores with a tableside fondue fountain. Talk about gluttony overload. The whole place is like a luxury cartoon and I love it."

The Forge Restaurant has an interesting history. In historical terms, it is as iconic as Joe's Stone Crab and Tobacco Road in influence, notoriety, and age. The building as an entity has been around since the twenties, when blacksmith Dino Phillips opened a forge on

41st Street. He designed iron gates and sculptures for the homes of Miami's elite. It was easier to be entrepreneurial in those days, and Phillips eventually converted his forge into a restaurant and casino. The Forge has been slinging great steak and attracting celebrities, politicians, and high society ever since. Famous regulars included Jackie Gleason, Frank Sinatra, Judy Garland, Meyer Lansky, Desi Arnaz, Elizabeth Taylor, Richard Nixon, and most recently, Madonna, Bill Clinton, Mickey Rourke, Elaine Lancaster, Justin Timberlake, and Jessica Biel.

Alvin Malnik, a prominent Miami Beach lawyer, purchased the restaurant in 1968 and completely remodeled it, a feat that took one year and included the addition of the new restaurateur's expansive art and antiques collection. This would not be the first makeover for the restaurant. Malnik has friends in high places; he is even the godfather of Prince Michael II, aka Blanket, Michael Jackson's child. The turning point for the restaurant occurred in 1983, when Baron Philippe de Rothschild gifted Malnik a collection of his turn-of-the-century bottles, turning the famed Wine Cellar into one of the finest rare-wine collections in the world, containing more than 300,000 vintages. Local spirits writer Galena Mosovich tweeted: "Touring @theforgerestaurant's wine collection was overwhelmingly amazing. More than 70,000 bottles (what?!)—some dating back to the 1820s. There is a Chateau Cheval Blanc #1947 (good year)."

In the early nineties, Shareef Malnik, Alvin's son, who grew up in the restaurant, became the owner. Even more connected than his father, he brought additional allure to the establishment. The most recent temporary closing came in 2009, reopening with Chef Dewey LoSasso in 2010. The same year, Miami Beach mayor Matti Bower proclaimed April 27 "The Forge Day."

"I did want to point out, however, that while The Forge has been an iconic Miami restaurant for decades, they always have their eye on the future," says public relations rep Jessica Bishop. "Aside from adding in the latest in wine technology [ten Enomatic wine dispensers] to better showcase their cellar, they also recently hired Michelin-starred Executive Chef Christopher Lee to helm the kitchen. Chef Lee launched a new menu a few weeks ago that has gotten great praise from local critics. It is not just an 'out with the old in with the new' mentality; it is more thinking of proper ways to stay relevant in the Miami market."

For regular folks, The Forge is a fancy spot, the kind of place you save for special occasions or if you just want a night of upscale living. It remains with that part of Miami's history that is luxuriously excessive. Their Friday Veuve Clicquot happy hours are a standby favorite. And the decor, oh, the decadent decor! From the outside it looks like a grand old European palace; inside there is an abundance of wood paneling, crystal chandeliers, and luxurious and rich accents like mosaic glass windows, candles, and plush cushions that match the equally decadent menu of caviar, prime rib, foie gras, lobster, risotto, and truffles.

"Because it is located in a kind of nonglamorous section of Miami Beach, it manages to be good without depending on being trendy. It is not in South Beach. It is not at the Fontainebleau. It is just in Miami Beach, which means locals will go there, too," says Matt Meltzer. And really, that is all you need.

FOX'S SHERRON INN

6030 S. DIXIE HWY. • SOUTH MIAMI, FL 33143

(305) 661-9201

A Fox Walks into a Bar . . .

Scratch that—Betty Fox did not simply walk into the bar; she created the concept, opened, and ran the place until 1967. Located in South Miami and off the traditional tourist route, Fox's Sherron Inn continues to be an institution for locals and tourists alike.

Opened in 1946, rumor has it that Fox submitted the paperwork for the restaurant and bar in 1939, but World War II put her plans on hold. It originally was a liquor store and sandwich shop and looked much different than it does now. The room on the right-hand side facing US 1 housed the original liquor store, and the kitchen was located where the bar is now. The entrance also used to be in the front, but the expansion of US 1 took that over and moved it to the back. Can you image that? Eventually, it was time for Betty Fox to move on. George Andrews, a pilot for Pan Am Airways, bought the restaurant in 1967 and owned it until 2009, when current owner Rene Dahdah took over.

The restaurant was named Sherron for Fox's daughter, Sharon. The printers messed up the spelling of her name, but they decided not to fix it. Another interesting fact is that the complex is not a hotel. They used the word "inn" in the old definition of the word, which means inviting. Fox did live upstairs, but that is the extent of it. It is funny, during Ultra Music Festival time, the restaurant receives about seven calls a day inquiring about available rooms.

"Betty's father used to own many bars around downtown, so she grew up in the business," says general manager Ricardo Gutierrez. "It is one of the few places around here that existed in the fifties, and it was known to be a clandestine spot for its underground ambience, providing a one-stop shop for wheelings and dealings."

I could have also begun this chapter with a riddle. What do a fox, Ray Liotta, and a bar have in common? As a former University of Miami student, the actor is a regular when in town and notes in various interviews that the spot never changes.

Walking into the dark restaurant is a shock to the eyes. The main room is always pitch-black. There is one small front window, but it always remains covered, no matter the hour. Reading menus by candlelight or cellphone is normal. If you ever need to hide out, they probably won't find you here. The restaurant is divided into three rooms. The main room is cozy, with circular black banquette booths and an old-fashioned, manly wood bar that features a fox mosaic on the wall and strong drinks. The two back rooms are completely different and feature regular dining tables, with exposed brick walls, fancy

chandeliers, and tiled black-and-white-patterned floors. The room on the left-hand side, or the front of the restaurant if looking in from US 1, features a large window and is the room that receives the largest amount of natural light. The entire establishment boasts an overall old-fashioned, speakeasy style. Before smoking was outlawed, it was dense with cigarette smoke.

Fox's is the oldest establishment with a dual liquor license in Miami, capable of operating a liquor store and bar at the same time. The liquor store, which can be found in the back, can remain open until 5 a.m. by law, but these days it closes at 2 a.m., still later than other liquor stores around. It has always functioned as a walk-up liquor store.

On September 1, 1977, the *Miami News* featured a fantastic human-interest story about a deaf-mute gentleman that worked as a dishwasher at Fox's. Unfortunately, a car hit him, but George Andrews was by his side throughout the entire ordeal. The gentleman even rented a room from the owners, further emphasizing the strong bonds the restaurant promotes.

From the jukebox to the live bands, music has always been a mainstay of Fox's. These days, the banquettes can easily be moved to create an open-floor format for bands to play and the crowd to dance or mosh. All steel and chrome, the famous jukebox is currently being repaired, but in its heyday it played it all. In 2010 a popular night was Shuffle Tuesdays, when music was devoted to the Smiths. It was called "A Night of the Smiths" and included two-for-one drinks.

The newest owners have made some tweaks to the menu, but here is a little-known secret: Customers that want the old menu can ask for it. We always have some liverwurst in the back. Tuesday and Thursday nights are prime rib night, but my favorite night is Friday. Oh, that pan-fried snapper is absolutely delicious.

"We have customers that come every day, some even up to two times a day. Many of our standby regulars do not like the changes that we have made, but they keep on coming back for the experience and the people. As for the die-hard customers, sometimes we will get a family after a funeral or a death anniversary come in to honor the person because it was their favorite place. Our main goal now is trying to sell an old concept to a new generation of Fox's lovers."

FRANKIE'S PIZZA

9118 BIRD RD. • MIAMI, FL 33156

(305) 298-4609 • FRANKIESPIZZAONLINE.COM

Miami's Oldest Pizza Shop

*L*ike any other metropolitan city, Miami is littered with pizza shops. There is one on practically every corner. From high end to cheap and quick, New York style, Napolitana, or *al taglio*, there is a pizza for every taste.

Unlike most pizzas, Miami's oldest is *al taglio* style, with a thin crust that is chewy and crunchy. *Al taglio* means "by the cut" in Italian and is usually square or rectangular in shape. At Frankie's, not much has changed since its opening. The Jetsons futuristic-style light-up sign still shines, the friendly customer service remains the same, and, of course, the pizza has always been and will always be square. It is stuck in a time capsule because it has never steered from the Pasquarella way. With accolades like *Bon Appétit*'s "Top 8 Gourmet Pizza Shops in America" (1994, 1995) and *Miami New Times*' "Best Pizza of Miami" (1997, 2007), it is no wonder the pizza slingers are still around. The pizza has such a cult following that local Carlos Becerra even filmed a documentary about the late owner titled *Following Frank: Saucy Intonations of Miami's Pizza King*.

Opened by Frank and Doreen Pasquarella on Valentine's Day 1955, the pizzeria has been a family-owned favorite since its inception. Originally from Ohio, the couple was honeymooning in Miami when they noticed an abundance of Italian restaurants, but few pizza shops. This decade saw an increased interest in ethnic cuisines due to returning soldiers craving the foods they enjoyed abroad while at war. In this case, it was Italian food that had Miami hungry. In tow with an original recipe from Frankie's mother, the couple quickly relocated to Miami to fill the pizza void.

Originally located on US 1 inside a Norman Brothers Produce Store and across the street from the University of Miami, the pizza shop catered to the university's many students. But at $175 per month, the rent was too high for the owners, and two years later they moved to their current location on the historic Bird Road. In terms of business, there was not much else on Bird Road at the time. Renee, one of Pasquarella's daughters, recalls the Miami of yesterday, when she was a child growing up at Frankie's: "Miami ended around 107th Avenue. When we were little kids, there was a horse post outside of the store; it was all dirt roads and cows crossed the streets on a regular basis. Kendall was nothing but tomato fields. Now, there are businesses all around us and Bird Road is one of Miami's most congested main arteries. Two more things: We have always been closed on Mondays, and we have always been a cash-only business."

Frank and Doreen have passed on, but Renee and Roxanne Pasquarella continue the Frankie's legacy. Roxanne's son, Christopher, works at the shop as well and is the next key to continuity. At times, there are hurdles to running a family business. Because they are not a large corporation, the economic recession hit them hard. To combat this, they introduced a food truck of the same name in order to redistribute employees, which are like family, and bring in more

Vintage Spot
REY'S PIZZA: EST. 1980S

Rey is the Spanish word for "king," and this pizza is fit for a Miami king. Channel the flavors of Cuba in pizza form, topped with a secret sauce and mozzarella and Gouda cheeses. Pizza is not the only thing on the menu; you can order a side of mamey milkshake and Cuban sandwiches with your Cuban treat.

2381 W. Flagler St.; (305) 232-5550; reypizza.com

money while giving back to the community. The truck helps the pizzeria participate in events that were previously a hassle due to lack of transportation and equipment.

Renee is passionate about pizza, the pizzeria, and life in general. "We still place a free, hot slice of pizza on top of every box so our customers can enjoy it on the way home, just like our dad did," she says. "One day, the mixer at Godfather's Pizza down the street from us broke down and we lent one to them. Our dad always encouraged us to always check out the competition. We love to support other pizza places, and competition is healthy because without it, you become complacent. I love pizza, and I like to see what else is out there. Locally, I like Mike's Irish Pub on Venetian Causeway; it truly is one of my favorites, besides Frankie's, of course. If you ever go to Fort Lauderdale, check out Riverwalk Pizzeria."

What makes a good pizza? "I loved our pizza growing up because we use and still use fresh ingredients. In the past, companies have approached us for franchising opportunities, but we have always refused. The first thing they want to do is cut costs, and cutting costs means less fresh ingredients and a lower-quality product. We do not cut corners. Also, our preparation process takes longer than other pizza shops. We know that we need to turn over a lot of pizza, and that is fine and we will continue doing that because a lot of love goes into making the pies. Frankie's is like a family member to all of us, and for it to close would be like a death in the family."

HIALEAH PARK RACING & CASINO

2200 E. FOURTH AVE. • HIALEAH, FL 33013
(305) 885-8000 • HIALEAHPARKCASINO.COM

The Grand Dame

J had my junior and senior homecoming dances at Hialeah Park Racing & Casino," says Cari Garcia, local food blogger and Hialeah native. "In the past few years, it has seen a bit of a revival with the return of the horse races and as the official home of the revamped Hialeah Fair. For the better part of my life, it stood as a mostly empty and dilapidating behemoth that Hialeahans I know do not have a connection to. And before 2013, it was always up in the air as to whether or not it would be demolished."

Hialeah Park Racing & Casino is a mammoth of an establishment. Known as "The World's Most Beautiful Race Course," it serves a variety of purposes over 200 acres of land. First and foremost, it is a horse racetrack, but it is also an event space, a proper park, a food court, an Audubon Society–sanctioned flamingo habitat, a National Register of Historic Places property, and, as of 2013, a casino.

The history of this institution is magnificent and dates back to twenties with the beginnings of the city of Hialeah. Founded by Glenn Curtiss and James Bright, Hialeah, aka "The City of Progress, was created on the same principles as other cities in the greater Miami-Dade County area: the dream of creating one's own city in the heart of America's newest playground for a quick profit. The park opened to the public in 1925 as the Miami Jockey Club. Historical research shows that the opening received more coverage in the Miami media than any other sporting event in the history of the city up to that time. Not even one year later, the Hurricane of 1926 caused great devastation around the city and especially to the newly opened park. To recover

from the destruction, it was sold to Joseph Widener, who, with the help of architect Lester Geisler, made it the illustrious estate that it is today.

In its heyday Hialeah Park was the best of the best. Its elaborate design—with intricate details like terrazzo floors, stone archways, grand staircases, and junglelike bougainvilleas—was inspired by the great estates of both this country and Europe, all evident from the moment you drive up to the palatial porte cochere. Fancy, famous folk such as Frank Sinatra, Winston Churchill, John F. Kennedy, Joe DiMaggio, and Amelia Earhart walked its halls and their portraits grace the walls—oh, if walls could talk! But it does not stop there: Even the famous horses of the day ran on the track, including War Admiral, Citation, Carry Back, Forego, Seattle Slew, and, of course, Seabiscuit. In 1938 Widener introduced the famous flamingos. This is a spectacle unlike anything you have ever seen. The flamingos, which were originally imported from Cuba, live in the park and perform

"The Flight of the Flamingos" on race day, usually before the feature race.

The park's downhill spiral began in 1972, when for the first time in its history, it lost the prime winter racing dates to newer and more popular racetracks like Gulfstream Park and Calder Race Course, which feature more prominent locations and newer facilities, leaving Hialeah Park in the dust. Shortly thereafter, the property changed hands again with the purchase by northerner and real estate giant John Brunetti. Its future appeared bleak, and many believed it was destined for demolition to make space for high-rises. Then, the incredible occurred. In 1979 Hialeah Park was designated a National Historic Landmark. Unfortunately, that still did not bring much glory back to the establishment, but it did save it from demolition. In 2001 the last thoroughbred race was held at the park and it closed for a period of eight years, opening again in 2009 with quarter horse races.

Though it has had a tumultuous past, 2013 brought renewed life to the dilapidating estate with renovations and the addition of the casino. A second phase will bring a hotel, a movie theater, and an outlet-shopping village.

But still, many things need to be taken into consideration. In its glory days, Hialeah was a gauche city that attracted the rich and famous. Through the fifties the city stood as a symbol of progress and beamed like the illustrious golden child it was. After the Cuban Revolution at opening of the sixties, the mass waves of Cuban exiles dramatically changed Miami's demographics; a large portion settled in Hialeah and completely changed the aesthetics and theme of the city from a vacation spot to a working-class industrial enclave. Other national changes, such as the end of the passenger train era, also greatly affected the park. Since that time a negative stereotype has loomed over the city, one that has been difficult to shed and one that will need to be shed in order for the park to return to its better days. And while the addition of the casino is a positive in certain respects, Garcia says that most of the players you see there are the old and retired spending the little money they receive from their Social Security checks, which cannot be good for the overall community.

For now, here are some vignettes from better times. On June 7, 1998, the *Boca Raton News* reported: "In its heyday, Hialeah Park would draw tens of thousands of people. The rich and famous considered it their playground. The lush gardens. Flowering vines crawling up outside walls. The breathtaking spectacle of flamingos circling high above the track before the daily feature race." On February 22, 2014, the *New York Times* recalled: "Palm Beach socialites arrived on the cushioned seats of special trains. Hialeah's annual opening was as big an event for society pages as for the sports sections. Men wore coats and ties; women donned jewelry and hats." With all the new improvements headed their way, many hope that the Park will return to those better times.

JACKSON SOUL FOOD

950 NW THIRD AVE. • MIAMI BEACH, FL 33136
(305) 374-7661 • JACKSONSOULDFOOD.COM

Overtown's Got Soul

*J*ackson Soul Food is an institution. Everyone in Overtown knows about it," says local activist and philanthropist Amy Rosenberg. "What sets it apart from all the other Southern food spots in town? It is authentic," adds local Malik Benjamin. "I am not some Bob's Big Boy–eating slob or some pretentious hipster foodie; my family is Carolinian so I know good Southern food and I understand and respect where it comes from. Even though it is not the best to eat, it damn sure is authentic and good. Fish and grits, red velvet cake, okra—delicious!"

Chitterlings, collard greens, fish and grits (they offer a special boiled fish and grits on Friday, Saturday, and Sunday), fried chicken, corn bread, biscuits, BBQ ribs, macaroni and cheese, sweet tea, peach cobbler, and carrot cake are the makings of a great Southern meal, and Jackson Soul Food has been doling out the goods since 1946. Most popular are the catfish, biscuits, pancakes, and country bacon. Let us talk about this country bacon. This is not regular old bacon—it is marinated in cream, dusted in flour, and fried to perfection. And wait, let us not forget the mac and cheese. "My favorite dish at Jackson's has to be the mac and cheese," says Rosenberg. "I am a sucker for a bowl of cheesy goodness, and they do it right."

Johnny Mae Johnson originally opened the restaurant at St. John's Missionary Baptist Church at 1333 NW Second Ave. He then passed the restaurant to his brother, Demas, and his wife, Jesse, who in turn handed it to one of their twelve children, Shirlene Ingraham, current owner and manager. The restaurant has changed locations a

total of four times over the years, finally settling at its current location on NW Third Ave. This family affair is not going anywhere anytime soon. In the last few years, the area has been revived with help from the Overtown Community Redevelopment Agency, and Ingraham is a true community activist and preservationist. The food is so good that it could easily be found in any other part of town, but instead, she keeps it in Overtown. She also tries her best to employ people from the community as well as individuals who have records and cannot easily find employment elsewhere.

A historically African-American community in Miami, Overtown is often referred to as the Harlem of the South and was originally established as Colored Town. Landmarks that are still around to this day include the Lyric Theater, Miami's first theater, and the Dorsey House, the reconstructed home of the first black millionaire in Miami, D. A. Dorsey. At the height of its popularity in the forties and fifties, the likes of Aretha Franklin, Ella Fitzgerald, and Martin Luther King Jr. were a common sight in the community. When segregation was alive and well, black performers who played Miami Beach's top hotels and clubs made their way back to Overtown, the only area in which they could stay overnight in iconic hotels like the Dorsey, Mary Elizabeth, Sir John, Carver, and Wisteria. After-hours parties and pop-up concerts were all the rage. It was a thriving community, with tons of nightclubs and restaurants and all sorts of commerce, most owned by blacks. Opened at the peak of the action, Jackson Soul Food was at the heart of it all.

In the sixties, as Miami's population increased twofold, expansion from downtown prompted the building of two expressways, which tore the community of Overtown apart. Prior to this, Overtown was a large, vibrant community and its heart was on Seventh Avenue, which is now a highway exit ramp. Despite the influx of ethnic groups from Central and South America and the Caribbean, Miami is still a city of the South, and segregation was very much alive for a better part of the twentieth century. But, those who visit Overtown today can see that there is something positive brewing, and it is slowly being reconstructed to its former glory days.

A true testament to the soul of a restaurant is its owner. Ingraham is there daily at 6 a.m., cooking the food for the day to come. "It is a special place because of the owner Shirlene," says Rosenberg. "She is an amazing woman—caring, devoted to her staff and her community. She is usually in the kitchen when I go there, and I always ask the servers if she can come out for a quick hug."

The restaurant previously had strange hours, from 6 a.m. to 1 p.m., focusing on great breakfast food and early lunches, but demand has changed (it's now open from 5:30 a.m. to 7:00 p.m.) and they have changed with it for the betterment of the community. The restaurant's decor leaves much to be desired, but lets the food shine above all. The centerpiece is a horseshoe counter similar to S&S Diner's, and its walls are a nod to the community's history, featuring an abundance of framed black-and-white photos.

The restaurant is also involved in the music realm, all for the benefit of the community. "Food and music are the two best ways to bring people together," says Rosenberg, who is also the director of the Overtown Music Project, a nonprofit that celebrates the music, history, and spirit of this town in its heyday. "Overtown Music Project nights with the likes of Bobby Stringer (RIP), Treetop, and Joey Gilmore makes me feel like I am back in the heyday," says Benjamin. Over the years, these chic events have attracted a large following of swanky guests not only from Overtown, but from all over the city.

JAZID

1342 WASHINGTON AVE. • MIAMI BEACH, FL 33139

(305) 673-9372 • JAZID.NET

Incubator of Local Music

*A*s the name implies, Jazid opened as a jazz lounge in June 1996. Original owners Cesare Mazzoli and Michelle McKinnon moved to Miami in the nineties at the height of Miami Beach's glitzy revival—think nightclubs, models, Madonna, and Versace. From the very beginning, Jazid was meant to be a locals' spot and a departure from Miami Beach's overpriced cocktails, long lines, and bad service.

A former model herself, Michelle was the lounge's unofficial spokesperson. A 1996 article in *Ocean Drive* details the early life of Jazid: "She [Michelle] was the decorator of the spot. The club has been modeled on the old-fashioned jazz room concept—a smoky, candlelit, intimate atmosphere. 'People are really comfortable here—the regulars walk in and say hi to each other now and I love that,' she says." Jazid's early days featured such bands as Caesars' Jade Chapter 11, Joey Gilmore and Betty Padgett, and the Billy Marcus Trio.

Remember the popular Ruby Cocktail from *Sex and the City* (circa 2002)? A little-known fact: A former Jazid bartender named Carla created a twist on the original version of the cocktail. An immediate hit, it was picked up by television executives and featured on the show. The recipe consists of 6 ounces of Florida ruby-red grapefruit juice mixed with 3 ounces of citrus vodka, shaken with ice, strained into a sugar-rimmed martini glass, and garnished with a slice of fresh grapefruit.

In 2003 the original owners moved on and local DJ Daniel Wohlstein took over. Many have credited Daniel with doing an excellent job

of preserving the original soul of Jazid. Being the boss has not taken away from his first passion, as he still frequently DJs upstairs on Saturdays. Over the years the lounge has expanded from strictly jazz to include funk, cumbia, reggae, rock, deep house, funk, and hip-hop for an overall global and eclectic mix, better embodying the essence and culture of the local community.

The two-story dimly lit lounge features a unique atmosphere with two completely different ambiences. The downstairs area is the typical dive lounge that offers seating, a dance floor, a bar, and a music stage for reggae and rock bands to jam. The upstairs area is a colorful and cozy living room–style setting with a pool table and DJ area. On quiet nights, the upstairs area is great for private rendezvous. The lounge's interiors are vibrantly dressed with works by local artist David Le Batard, more commonly known as LEBO.

Jazid is the only spot on Miami Beach that remains solely dedicated to live music. For the local music scene, it has been instrumental. If it were not for this South Beach live-music mainstay, many

Miami bands probably would have never gotten their shot. PALO!, Spam Allstars, Locos Por Juana, Suénalo, Xperimento, Jahfe, and Art-Official have all played at Jazid.

"Jazid does what no other local venue has achieved; they feature live music—and very interesting DJs upstairs—virtually every night of the week," says local musician Steve Roitstein of PALO! "This provides a place for musicians and music fans to interact in a town lacking in live-music venues. This is particularly rare on Miami Beach, where the emphasis is usually placed on genres such as EDM and hip-hop. Jazid provides a place for local bands to perform, build an audience, develop their sound, and hone their craft. It is laid-back, low pressure, and informal, which fits perfectly with Miami's original Latin fusion bands. The commitment that Jazid has made to live, original music in South Florida is unmatched. I would go as far to say that without Jazid, it is possible that at least a couple of our amazing local bands would not have been able to develop the way they did. That is how important Jazid has been to our scene."

According to Tony Alarcon, another local musician and managing partner at Jazid, "Miami is the northernmost city in Latin America, and we aim to embody that in all aspects. On Miami Beach, places come and go too frequently. If you do not establish an identity and stick to your guns, you are a goner. Jazid is Miami personification at its finest, the meshing of all cultures, which is what the city is all about. If walls could talk, this place has a million stories. My favorite night was when Prince showed up. A local band was playing upstairs and he comes out of nowhere, demanding a guitar to play with them. The legendary Prince, folks! I love that it has always been and will always be a true locals' spot. If you are visiting from out of town and know a local, you are most likely going to end up here or one of our chill counterparts—Mac's Club Deuce, Ted's Hideaway, or Purdy Lounge. Aside from the [Mac's Club] Deuce, we are the oldest kids on the beach block. People from all walks of life love us, and not many places can say that. Plus, we have cheap drinks, another unheard-of thing on the beach, especially since Zeke's Roadhouse closed down. As for me, I used to play here; now I am a part owner. Life takes you down some interesting roads."

JOE'S STONE CRAB

11 WASHINGTON AVE. • MIAMI BEACH, FL 33139

(305) 673-0365 • JOESSTONECRAB.COM

Miami Culinary Classic

*A*s much as I have been into food all my life, I learned all I needed to know about Joe's from my father. From one fatherly figure to another, this is his ode to the father of stone crabs: "I have always had a liking for Joe's and suspect that Joe knew that the South of Fifth neighborhood would be popular one day. I love Joe's location because it's right at the beginning of Miami Beach, easy to get to, and you do not even have to traipse the congested streets of Collins and Washington. The parking is equally great; there are many options nearby and it is safe. For anyone that lives in Miami, easy parking is of great importance. I especially love the impeccably dressed tuxedoed waiters that waltz around with large trays of fresh and vibrantly colored stone crabs—truly beautiful imagery. On the way out, I suggest grabbing a matchbook; even if you do not smoke, you are now part of the Joe's club. On my way home, with a belly full of stone crabs, I indulge in the great night I had as I pass over the MacArthur Causeway, watching the rows of cruise ships that await their turn to disembark and the bright lights of downtown Miami, Joe's in the background."

Everyone knows Joe's, and it is usually at the top of everyone's Miami list. No trip to Miami is complete without a visit to this iconic restaurant, even if it is just for a slice of key lime pie from Joe's Take Away. In operation since 1913, there are countless books and articles about the family, the restaurant, the menu, and even the waiters. Like Delmonico's and Peter Luger's in New York, Joe's is a cult classic known the world over and popular with anyone that enjoys stone

crabs, key lime pie, fried chicken, or keeping up with the Joneses. The likes of Al Capone, J. Edgar Hoover, Bill Clinton, George W. Bush, Andy Garcia, Madonna, Dwayne Wade, and many, many others have passed through its doors. Maybe even you, fine reader!

Located in the South of Fifth neighborhood, Joe's Stone Crab has expanded to become a compound of sorts, including the restaurant's many dining rooms, Joe's Take Away, the shipping area, and even a dry-cleaning area. The restaurant is set in the style of a rustic fish house and is large, with room upon room of tables with linens and terrazzo and wood floors. Servers are clad in impeccable tuxedos. Joe's accepts no reservations, so there is always a mob scene outside its doors. Friday and Saturday nights herald wait times of up to two or three hours. The best advice is to arrive right when the restaurant opens for dinner at 5 p.m. Stone crab season runs October 15 through May 15. In the off-months, Joe's Take Away shuts down and the restaurant only serves dinner. Stone crab prices have changed through the years. When Joe's first opened, they charged 75 cents for four or five crabs; now they are upwards of $79.95 for a serving of five or six claws.

Miami Beach started out as a barrier island filled with swamp rats and thick mangroves. The island was meant to be a large coconut and avocado tree plantation, but failed attempts relegated it to a paradise resort and real estate haven. In 1915 John Collins, the Lummus brothers, and Carl Fisher incorporated the City of Miami Beach with 300 residents. Joseph "Joe" and Jennie Weiss were among them. An early settler and food pioneer, Joe Weiss began as a waiter in New York and moved to Miami, like many others, to cure his health ailments. The couple purchased a bungalow and began slinging food from their front porch under the name Joe's Restaurant. They would not serve the infamous stone crab for another decade, but offered popular items like snapper, pompano, crawfish, and mackerel—common local fare.

A *Sarasota Herald-Tribune* article from May 15, 1977, explained it perfectly: "Joe's Stone Crab—Where an unwanted beach pest was turned into a gourmet's delight." It was the first time anyone had placed stone crabs on a menu, and their success continues more than a hundred years later—success that can be attributed to a lucky accident of being at the right place at the right time.

A builder named James Allison, in the boom era, brought in a team of ichthyologists to classify the creatures found in the waters around Miami. The stone crabs bore a strong resemblance to the European stone crabs found in the waters of the North Atlantic and the fjords of Scandinavia. Joe had one of his cooks, Horatio Johnson, boil some up in the back of the house. The first batch tasted of heavy iodine, but rather than throw them out, he chilled them on ice naturally removing the metallic taste. In terms of continuity, the stone crab's claws are self-replenishing. Catch a stone crab, detach one of its claws, return the crab to the sea, and the next year it will have grown a new claw. It is illegal to catch or take a stone crab during breeding and regenerating season, which is between May and October.

Here are some fun, little-known facts: The oldest dish on Joe's menu is the coleslaw, a recipe of Jennie Weiss's. The apple pie was the first dessert on the menu. The key lime pie is equally famous; Joe's granddaughter, Joann, created it.

More recently, Deeny Kaplan Lorber wrote *Waiting at Joe's*, a book about the famous service staff at Joe's Stone Crab, and not about the infamous wait. And while Joe is important, it is the waitstaff that makes it what it is today, and Lorber did a great job of highlighting the history of the restaurant through a new set of eyes. A running theme in this own book, Joe's has never stopped being a family-run institution. It is a recipe for success.

One last piece of advice, from my father: "Don't bother with the menu, and just order the stone crabs."

LA CASA DE LOS TRUCOS

1343 SW EIGHTH ST. • MIAMI, FL 33135

(305) 858-5029 • CRAZYFORCOSTUMES.COM

Nobody Does Weird So Well

ommy, mommy, look at that scary mask!" shrieks child number one. "I want to be a princess," sings child number two, pulling the aforementioned mommy in the opposite direction. This is a common scene at La Casa de los Trucos, Miami's costume shop mecca. Located on colorful Calle Ocho amid open-air fruit markets, restaurant ventanitas, and Mexican restaurants, this is not the typical spot for a costume store, especially one that has been around since 1973. But then again, this is Little Havana and anything goes, the store adding an extra jolt of eccentricity and play to an already colorful street.

The store's iconic name literally translates to "The House of Tricks" and with good measure, since they have about 15,000 tricks up their sleeve. Little surprises such as rubber snakes and fake rattraps lurk around each corner, making for a fun house experience. "When you come to our store, we will show you magic tricks and make-up prosthetics. We will shock you, squirt you, and give you scars—fake of course," says owner, Jorge Torres.

Outside, a pack of wooden monsters and superheroes guard the store from criminals (and possibly naughty children) and greet guests. The cavelike interior is small, but every nook and cranny, even the ceiling, is utilized to feature costume products. The store is open year-round, but Halloween is when it gets the most traction. There are lines out the door all October long.

In terms of product, La Casa de los Trucos has it all, from the quintessential sexy police costume to special-effects makeup that would make Quentin Tarantino proud, fake parking tickets, and glitter

and masks. "La Casa de los Trucos is a local store, and we were around way before any of the current party stores," Torres says. "I think it is important to note that we reinvest in our community and are not simply a temporary or pop-up store from another state. We are also not a party store that sells party supplies, but a costume and props specialty store that has often been described as a costume compound. We sell magic tricks, traditional costumes, sexy costumes, costumes for dogs and cats, accessories, hats, weapons, masks, makeup, wigs, bridal and baby shower items, headpieces, and masquerade masks. We also rent large and elaborately detailed seasonal costumes such as the Easter Bunny and Santa Claus and even Purim costumes."

As for Torres's top costume picks, "I love them all, so it is hard for me to pin down favorites. For kids, I prefer superhero and princess costumes. For adults, I prefer zombie costumes; maybe I am watching too many zombie shows and movies."

The store originally opened in Cuba in the early twenties, but after the infamous Cuban Revolution, the family moved the store stateside to Little Havana. At almost one hundred years old, Torres claims that La Casa de los Trucos is one of the oldest costume stores in the world. "My father, Esteban Torres, opened the original store in Cuba. He brought it to Miami because, like most displaced Cubans, he wanted to create a memory of Havana here in the United States. The store was popular with kids in Cuba because of all the tricks and magic." The Little Havana store opened as a small wooden building on cinder blocks, and the family built a bigger location in the same spot in 1980. Now, they have two buildings warehousing over 15,000 different styles of costumes.

As for the original store in Cuba, it no longer exists, as the reign of Fidel Castro banished most holiday celebrations. Interestingly enough, in more recent years, the island has seen a minor shift and micro costume stores have sporadically resurfaced. A *BBC News* article from November 1, 2013, highlighted such festivities from the island nation: "The privately-run Shangri-la club was the first to throw a Halloween party last year: manager Sergio said Cubans were recovering things from past generations. This year, even Havana University was celebrating."

Prior to the reign of Castro, elaborate dress of all types were popular, and in the society scene, it was extremely common for young girls and women to receive shipments of the finest clothes direct from France and beyond. Style inspirations of the day included a young Celia Cruz, Alba Marina, and Olga Chorens. For the men, it was Meyer Lansky and Desi Arnaz. All were classics of the time.

"Little Havana offers a great vantage point for the state of Miami's economics and population and tourism trends." says Torres. "The neighborhood is the heart and soul of our culture, where we came from. We have sadly seen a whole bunch of our retail peers come and go, but some of my favorites like Los Piñarenos Fruteria and King's Ice Cream still run strong. We have generations of loyal customers and love seeing the generational continuance; kids that grew up coming to the store now bring their own children as adults. It is a special feeling."

You can go to Party City like everyone else or go to La Casa de los Trucos, turning out unique and original costumes that are sure to get you compliments. The store is one of those places that everyone just knows about. Most kids in Miami-Dade County, no matter how far away they lived or what nationality they were, grew up as a customer of La Casa de los Trucos and can recall that special costume upon inquiry—it may even still take up space in their closet, they are that good.

LA EPOCA

200 E. FLAGLER ST. • MIAMI, FL 33131

(305) 374-7731 • LAEPOCA.COM

Miami's Boutique Department Store

Department stores were 20th-century landmarks of urban life," according to Jan Whitaker in *Service and Style: How the American Department Store Fashioned the Middle Class*. "As they developed early in the century, department stores became core institutions, which reassured Americans by their very existence that life was good, that beauty mattered, and that order and stability prevailed. Through displays, demonstrations, lectures, and entertainment

spectacles, the stores defined a way of life while furnishing the necessities and luxuries that it entailed."

These are the words Brian and Randy Alonso live by as they continue the legacy of La Epoca. Self-described as downtown Miami's boutique department store, La Epoca is the city's only remaining independent department store. Opened in September 1965, it has outlived Burdines, the beloved original Florida store, and popular downtown non-local haunts such as Woolworth's and Sears. The future is bright for La Epoca. In 2014 a new specialty store focusing on American denim will open inside the historic Alfred Dupont Building, where its journey originally began.

La Epoca has a long history in both Miami and Cuba. The store was originally founded in 1885 in Havana, the country's capital city, as a small fabric store. Emigrating from Spain, brothers Diego and Angel Alonso took over the store in 1927 with dreams of expansion. At the onset of the Cuban Revolution in the early sixties, the store was confiscated by Fidel Castro and to this day is still operated by the government. Exiled to Miami, the brothers decided to replicate the store, and La Epoca opened inside the Alfred Dupont Building in downtown Miami.

In 2005 the store moved to its current location at 200 East Flagler St. A historical spot previously serving as the location of Miami's first Walgreens, it featured a soda fountain and lunch counter called The Rail, where the most important and trendy of the day lunched. The building's exterior features a protected facade in the Art Deco style that is specifically Art Moderne. With over 25,000 square feet, La Epoca sells men's, women's, and children's apparel; footwear; luggage; and accessories. It is the only store in downtown Miami to carry luxury brands such as Hugo Boss, Diesel, 7 For All Mankind, Scotch and Soda, Christian Dior, Lanvin, Chanel, and Yves Saint Laurent.

As with many other stories in this book, this is a tale of the immigrant dream fulfilled. What is even more interesting is that most of the staff has been around for decades; most are in their later years and like family. The staff is reminiscent of the grandparent who knows best, offering advice on fit and styling. How can you say no to grandma or grandpa?

In the seventies, Miami's population grew in size due to the previous decade's mass influx of immigrants from south of the border.

While much of Miami's population moved to the suburbs, a flow of international travelers from Venezuela, Argentina, and Colombia provided an increase of 40 percent in sales across all stores in downtown Miami, offsetting the expected loss. "These travelers' only interests were shopping and Disney World, in that order," says Brian Alonso. To satisfy the masses, the stores stayed open until 10 p.m.

Naturally, La Epoca has experienced its downs. Being in the heart of downtown Miami is a hard feat for any store to carry out, much less a department store. "The best years of downtown Miami were seen between 1979 and 1983," Alonso continues. "Shortly after the devaluation of the Venezuelan currency, we noticed a steep drop in sales. Locally, our Miami was in a state of transition and we could not count on the locals. Those were tough times."

The all-important question remains: How does an independent department store stay open in the face of mergers and consolidations? "This is a family store and will always be a family store," Alonso explains. "The second that changes is the second that the La Epoca name is lost. It is our values and the way we organize ourselves that has made this a continued success. It is also interesting to note that the fashion world functions differently. Sometimes, it is better to go to where the sales are least likely to occur." They could have moved to Dadeland Mall or any other prominent mall that has popped up over the years, but this is a true community store, never forgetting its roots.

The list of independent department stores is short. With only two examples in Florida, Bealls and Jacobson's, stores like these are a marvel. La Epoca is in a position where they are able to market to both locals and tourists. "History has a way of repeating itself," Alonso says. "We are experiencing a great influx of tourism. The cruise travelers that come in daily through the Port of Miami have only one goal in mind—shopping. Currently, Brazilians are our best shoppers."

Downtown Miami is experiencing a great renaissance since its decline in the seventies, eighties, and nineties—one that will bring much-needed prosperity to the stores that have made downtown Miami the lustrous city that it is. La Epoca is part of Miami's past, present, and future, both a spectator and a participant in the city's magnificent evolution.

LAURENZO'S ITALIAN MARKET

16385 W. DIXIE HWY. • NORTH MIAMI BEACH, FL 33160

(305) 945-6381 • LAURENZOSMARKET.COM

Old-World Italy in Miami

*T*here are so many things to say about this place, it is hard to know where to begin. Laurenzo's Italian Market is Miami's oldest Italian market. It is an institution, and it is always top of mind for foodies looking for gourmet and/or Italian food. This store set the tone for gourmet markets in the city. There is no Little Italy in Miami like in other parts of the country, but a large population of Italian expats do live here, mainly in Coral Gables and the downtown neighborhood of Brickell. The store is stuck not only in another time, but in another country. For those who have been to Italy, you will be transported there upon entering the store. For those who have not been to Italy, this is a close second.

The local alternative weekly *Miami New Times* is most famous for their yearly "Best Of" list, and Laurenzo's has managed to snag most of their superlatives in the food realm over the years—Best Delicatessen, Best Wine Store, Best Gourmet Grocery, Best Homemade Pasta, Best Italian Grocer, Best Cheese, Best Farmer's Market—and many were repeats.

The store is divided into three buildings: the grocery store, the banquet hall, and the farmers' market, which offers fresh fruits and vegetables seven days a week. There is also a cafe, bakery, pizzeria, and sandwich shop. In the middle of the grocery store is a small seating section that acts as the cafe. The store, while small, is a bit of a maze, and the cafe can be easy to miss. But once you find it, it is all red- and green-checkered tablecloths, very Little Italy New York.

Located on West Dixie Highway, which is a vein of a road similar to US 1, Laurenzo's is easy to miss if you have never been. Its taupe exterior with faded brown-red lettering leaves much to be desired, but everything changes the moment you step inside. In the grocery store, there is homemade pasta and prepared foods; imported Italian products like cheese, cured meats, olives, crackers, pasta, wine, and cooking ingredients; and all varieties of Kinder Chocolate (not Italian, but equally loved by Italians and Americans alike). Cannoli, pizza, tartelli, espresso, ziti, and tomato sauce that will make an Italian mama gasp. Laurenzo's features seventy-five assorted shapes and flavors of pastas as well as seventeen types of ravioli, all homemade. Even the employees have a thick Italian accent and will randomly shout a word or phrase in Italian. I will let your Italian dreams prance around a little more . . . Okay, back to reality.

Ben Laurenzo opened the store in 1954 along with his brother Achilles. Originally from upstate New York, they are both second-generation Americans. Ben fought in the navy during World War II and like many other soldiers decided to move to South Florida shortly after his return. War does a number on individuals, and life in sunny Florida is much more appealing and as a whole more carefree than cold upstate New York. The store is now owned and operated by third-generation Americans David and Carol Laurenzo, the patriarch's children, but Ben can still be found at the store every day.

The idea for the store came about in 1951, when Ben and his family began delivering authentic Italian and specialty products in a station wagon from Palm Beach to the Keys. In the fifties, Italian cuisine and general culture was at an all-time high in Miami, and Laurenzo's delivery service was an instant hit. A permanent store was the next logical step. According to David, back in the fifties the North Miami area was rich with Italians, and a niche needed to be filled.

Also interesting is that they do not forget their roots. Italians like their holidays, and keeping true to tradition, they celebrate holidays like the Festival of San Gennaro, the Feast Day of San Marcos, and many more. The December holiday season is when the store is busiest, and there are usually lines out the door. As most regulars would say, it is worth it.

Ian Phillips states it best in an article about the now-famous local store in the magazine *Myami*: "Mom and Pop stores are easy to find up around the northeast coast, especially in cities like New York and the wow factor is there, and they have a certain amount of importance, but none that equals what Laurenzo's means to our surf and sun community . . . That is how important a market that showcases food with history, nutrition, and great taste is to me and obviously to my fellow Floridians."

MAC'S CLUB DEUCE

222 14TH ST. • MIAMI BEACH, FL 33139

(305) 531-6200

The Ultimate Dive Bar

*T*he staff at Mac's Club Deuce is protective of their boss, the venerable Mac Klein. He can usually be found in the small back office, but is selective about whom he speaks to. I tried hard, but alas was not able to penetrate the force field. At ninety-nine years old, it is understandable. Either way, I have frequented the spot enough times over the years to truthfully describe the intricacies of this rare establishment.

Mac's Club Deuce originally opened as Club Deuce in 1926. Not much is known about original owner Harold Schwartz. Doing research for more information about Schwartz, I came upon a local forum discussion on Miami Beach 411 about Mac's Club Deuce. On May 15, 2009, swaps522 posted: "I did sell a lot of vital supplies to the bookies in the Deuce area. After lunch and a light libation, I would walk over to the Henrosa, Haddon Hall, White House, and Cardozo and sell the 'turf accountants' tons of pencils (no erasers allowed), 3x5 scratch pads, chalk, and erasers. Bookies had a separate room off the lobbies, with tables and chairs for clients, and a huge chalkboard on which the Boardman would write the results of horse races around the country. These forward thinking citizens of SoBe were the pioneers of simulcasting OTB [off-track betting] parlours of today. Anybody need a Royal TW ribbon? I have a ton of them."

Mac Klein, the bar's current owner and only the second in its history, took over in 1964 with the following famous story: At the same hour that Mac's daughter Zina was born, Schwartz lost his life in another corner of Mount Sinai Hospital. Fate has a wicked sense of humor. Mac purchased the bar a few days later.

Mac's Club Deuce is the type of place that your mother would advise against going. I am pretty sure when my own mother reads this, she is going to cringe. The term "dive bar" was coined in the 1800s; these establishments were typically located below street level away from the common population. In more modern times, it usually refers to a hidden bar with cheap drinks that welcomes all walks of life. Oh, and has a jukebox, always a jukebox.

Sandwiched between the busy Collins and Washington Avenues, Mac's is a dive bar through and through. The South Beach landmark offers an alternative to the alternative on the island of Miami Beach with its mundaneness of velvet ropes, discriminating bouncers, and overpriced drinks, where even some ice with a splash of Coca-Cola can easily set you back eight bucks.

As a dive bar, Mac's is a grimy place. "I started coming here after my friend got kicked out of Twist, it was the only place he was allowed. Twist is gross, this is worse. Thankfully, they lifted the ban after a couple of months," says local Washington Delgado.

But, that is the point, it is not meant to be pretty. A waft of ciga-rette smoke hits you before you even enter the door, and a hazy smoke cloud looms overhead the entire length of your stay. The bathrooms are just as disgusting as Churchill's Pub and a haven for illegal goings-on. A pool table sits in the middle of the room, also a legend itself, as the famous Jackie Gleason is said to have played on it. The other iconic piece of decor is the neon-pink naked lady on the top wall kicking her high heels in the air. The snake-shaped bar is flanked by bar stools, and most of the dark space is clad in dark wood. And the pièce de résistance is a TouchTunes jukebox, located next to the billiard table, that plays everything from the old classics to Britney Spears.

The bartenders may not always be nice, but the crowd is friendly, drinks are cheap, and there is happy hour daily, two-for-one from 8 a.m. to 7 p.m. For those who have been to the Clermont Lounge in Atlanta, Mac's vibe is similar, but a hundred times dirtier and no strippers dance on the bars.

And even with all the negatives, it is a must visit. Why, you ask? First, it has been around since your grandmother, and second, well, it is an experience like no other. It is Miami Beach's oldest bar and raved about by the likes of Anthony Bourdain, Cameron Diaz, Keith Richards, and Rachael Ray for its anonymous appeal. The bar was also a favorite of Al Capone and B.B. King.

Mac's Club Deuce is a frequent stop on all Crime in Miami tours. It is a good place to find trouble. Mac Klein recounted the days of the Cocaine Cowboys to Laurie Charles of the *Miami New Times* in a September 16, 2013, article: "We had locks on the door sometimes," recalls Klein. "It was a dangerous time in the sense that things happened here that have never happened before and thank God, will hopefully never happen again."

The great thing about dives is, well, you can find just about anyone there. On any given night or day, you can easily find hookers next to Brits watching a game, lonely old ladies, and strung-out dudes looking to score some smack.

Finally, why is it called the Deuce? According to the Miami Dade Preservation League, the name is derived from the bar's location at *222* 14th St. For those who want more of the Deuce, purchase *The Deuce Book*, a ninety-six-page collection of photographs taken by Deuce bartender Melissa Burley. The book comes sealed with a Deuce sticker, coaster, matchbook, and temporary tattoo for forty bucks.

MAINZER'S GERMAN DELI

12113 S. DIXIE HWY. • MIAMI, FL 33156

(305) 251-2060

Scheibe of Deutschland

*G*ruß, willkommen im shop" is something you may have heard back when Mainzer's first opened in 1972. Located in the village of Pinecrest on the main artery of US 1, the store enjoyed its heyday in the seventies when much of the area was still a farming community with a large population of German expats looking for warmer pastures.

The Cuban Revolution of the sixties brought a mass influx of displaced refugees to Miami, changing the demographics of entire neighborhoods across the city. Closer to Homestead than downtown Miami, Pinecrest experienced a population surge much later than the rest of the city. These migration patterns are a study of great interest to anthropologists and historians, as they are unlike anything that has ever been seen in other cities with large immigrant communities.

In 1992 Hurricane Andrew was the final straw for many of Pinecrest's residents, many of whom felt displaced not only tangibly, but also in soul. The hurricane ravaged Homestead and the outlying areas of Country Walk and Pinecrest. Approximately half of the German community moved on to Broward and West Palm Beach Counties and beyond. These days, few Germans live in the area.

For Germans wanting to get their fix of the homeland, there are a handful of spots in the city—Fritz & Franz Bierhaus, Hofbrau Beerhall, Schnitzel Haus, the Butcher Shop (a modern interpretation of German charcuterie), and, of course, Mainzer's German Deli, which is the only place in town that offers a deli and store with imported products from Germany itself. Other European countries like the Netherlands,

Hungary, Austria, and Poland are less likely to find the foods of their homelands in Miami and can find a piece of the mother country at Mainzer's as well.

Opened in 1972 by Elizabeth Strissel, a businesswoman from Germany, the store is named after the Rhineland-Palatinate state capital, Mainz. Eventually Elizabeth moved on, and Ronald and Cheryl Mainzer purchased the store in 1989. (The couple adopted the store's name as their own last name.) Ronald is German and Cheryl is a Miami native, but a descendant of a mishmash of European countries. And while the store has been around for four decades, it remains under the radar, a little-known gem that is a must visit for locals and tourists alike.

The epitome of the quaint mom-and-pop shop, the store is a foodie homage to the lands of Europe. Mainzer's Deli is every German immigrant's dream store, perfect for continuing the lifestyle of the old country in America. The decor is also a nod to the small European town stuck in time. The old-school deli signs that hang from the ceiling are faded, in that color that is more Eastern Germany than West. The little store is chock-full of breads, chocolates, cookies, cakes, jams, jellies, cooking pastes, pastas, coffees, wines, vinegars, oils, condiments, cooking spices, and sauces, all from the home country.

They also have fresh baked bread and pretzels every Saturday morning and a fully stocked meat case with liverwurst, teewurst, cold-smoked pork loin, kielbasa, kolbasz, weisswurst, and knackwurst. A small menu of reasonably priced sandwiches and mayonnaise-laden salads are available for those on the go. And do not forget the beer. Berliner Weisse, Bock, Hefeweizen, and Kölsch are all in the cooler. Even the magazines are in German, in case one needs to catch up on the tabloids from back home.

And while the prices are not unreasonable, they are pricier than nearby Fresh Market and Whole Foods, even though they do not stock the majority of Mainzer's unique traditional products. Then there is the problem of ALDI. While not in the immediate neighborhood, it is close enough to be a competitor. In Germany, ALDI is a well-known brand that revolutionized the grocery market business, selling products at discounted prices. Optimistically, Cheryl says that they have loyal customers that will gladly pay double for good German bread. But, like any other mom-and-pop store, they are worried that their time is running out. "I recently read an article about the demise of mom-and-pop shops in Europe, so no one is safe," says Cheryl.

The Mainzers are a nice couple; Ronald, a native German, is amiable. Cheryl handles the front of the house and Ronald, the back, but he prefers to be in the front to spend more time with his lovely wife. "The store is like my living room, my home, my life. We are going to continue to make it work as long as we possibly can," says Cheryl. Mainzer's German Deli is filled with decades of memories. And as people become more and more knowledgeable about food and increase their interest in other countries' food traditions, maybe this is the little store that could.

MAYA HATCHA

3058 GRAND AVE. • MIAMI, FL 33133

(305) 443-9040 • MAYAHATCHA.COM

Flower Power Lives in Coconut Grove

A lot happened in the late sixties and seventies—Nixon, Somoza, The Doors concert on Dinner Key where Jim Morrison exposed himself, and the rise of the hippie movement across the country, including locally in Coconut Grove.

The Grove, as it is most commonly referred to, is an important part of Miami's history. Miami's first village, Bahamians and Americans established it in 1825. As opposed to downtown Miami, the Grove was always laid-back and bohemian, an island-like paradise painted into Miami's landscape. And while corporations have tried to commercialize it, the village's independent spirit always rises above. In the fifties, it was one of the first places in the country to openly support the creative community as a viable economic resource.

When the seventies and its flower power movement rolled around, hippies from all across the country invaded the Grove, making local Peacock Park home base. The Grove's newest residents slept on the streets and ate freely from the public fruit-bearing trees. While the movement preached peace, love, and unity, it was a difficult time for the group, as they faced discrimination from police officers and local store owners, who did not want to hire them. The movement died and the majority of the hippie community moved on. The Grove has gone through many rebirths, always finding it difficult to combine the bohemian spirit with the rising corporate culture. Walking down the streets away from CocoWalk, one cannot help but notice the charm that the village exudes.

One store that continues the free-spirited vibe of the hippie movement into the twenty-first century is Maya Hatcha. A combination of languages, *Maya* is Mayan for "head" and *Hatcha* Spanish for "hatch." Opened in 1968 by sisters Vivian and Sylvia, Maya Hatcha has supplied Miami's residents with the very best in ethnic items from around the world for decades and is still considered one of the most unique stores in the city.

Originally from Guatemala, the sisters came to Miami at an early age. They both attended the University of Miami and opened the store while in school at the young ages of nineteen and twenty-one, respectively, at the height of hippie popularity. Vivian studied both economics and business, but realized early on that she did not want to participate in the career rat race to the top. Instead, she channeled her energies into the store. When the hippies abandoned the Grove, she did not go with them. At its high point, the store stretched across four storefronts. "I believe my success comes not only from my passion and perseverance, but also from my high-quality taste in picking out the best and most unique items," says Vivian.

Located in a prime spot in the Grove, across from the famed CocoWalk, the store is jam-packed with a bevy of products, and Vivian uses every inch of space to effectively showcase them. Walls,

tabletops, and racks are covered with clothing, colorful masks, knick-knacks, indigenous decor, jewelry, purses, art, incense, music, hats, and greeting cards. Intricate and colorful Guatemalan bedspreads stretch across one of the back walls, and the pièce de résistance—water buffalo sandals, the preferred shoe of hippies—are available for only $16. Patchouli has been her best seller for years now.

In the early days of the store, Vivian primarily stocked items from Guatemala, but as the years have progressed, she has changed course to include items from all over the world and stocks a large quantity of US-made clothing. "Fashion and trends work in cycles. In the seventies and eighties, Indian clothing and indigenous Guatemalan products were popular. These days, there is a movement towards US-made clothing and a high interest in home decor and indigenous products from Asia," says Vivian.

One unique item sold in her store is the Guatemalan Worry Doll. The following anecdote is included with the display of dolls: "According to legend, Guatemalan children tell one worry to each doll when they go to bed at night and place the dolls under their pillow. In the morning, the dolls have taken their worries away."

Nothing is intrinsically average in the store. Even the music from the sound system that accompanies the shopping experience has a story. Vivian's music of choice comes from a private label called Putumayo, founded by Dan Storper. Despising the bland musical choices available in stores, Storper set out to make a change with the creation of his eccentric record label. The CDs can be purchased at the store as well.

As a business leader with roots in the community, Vivian also likes to support other entrepreneurs. Most recently, she began carrying art by Guatemalan sculptor Luis Carlos. Eventually she would like to open her own art gallery separate from the store to nurture her love of art. And it may just come to fruition. In the eighties, Vivian owned another store, albeit short-lived, called Elektra, which catered to the punk style of the time. The store was best known for its hand-painted and embellished socks.

"It is the strangest thing. The store is extremely popular abroad. A tourist will come in and show me a guide in Portuguese or German with my store as a must visit while in Miami. No complaints here, I find it all fantastic and fascinating," says Vivian.

Vivian is passionate about her store. It is her home, her life. Her passion has kept the store alive even during hard economic times. She takes great care to find top-notch, quality products and everything has a purpose and a place. The unique, the eccentric, the durable, and the comfortable will always have a place at Maya Hatcha.

MIAMI TWICE

6562 BIRD RD. • MIAMI, FL 33155

(305) 666-0127 • MIAMITWICE.COM

Twice Is Nice

Shopping is fun, and with a myriad of options from malls to boutiques and specialty stores, Miami is a shoppers' paradise for locals and tourists alike. Millions of international travelers invade Miami every year for shopping excursions, but surprisingly the vintage store market is one that is dwindling locally. Recently, however, a slew of thrift and consignment stores have cropped up. Mary Holle, owner of Miami Twice, notes that many people do not know the difference between a vintage store, a consignment store, and a thrift store. "Do not confuse us with a consignment store or a thrift store; we are a vintage store that also sells a small quantity of contemporary boutique items."

A consignment store is a store that sells secondhand items on behalf of the original owner, who receives a percentage of the selling price. A thrift store is a store that sells secondhand clothes and other household goods for charity. A vintage store is a store that sells items that are at least one decade old. All products in the store are purchased, owned, and sold by the store, which is usually a private company.

Historically, vintage clothing is more expensive, and the best stores carry authentic, non-mainstream products that are in good condition and not too overpriced. "I am very picky and I do not buy just anything," says Holle. "Items with even the smallest of damage are not valuable. In one second, I can tell you if a product is great or not. This is what I was meant to do and I am great at it." That type of integrity and attention to detail is what keeps Miami Twice above the competition.

Miami Twice is one of the smartest and oldest vintage stores in town. From the rare and vintage to the modern and unique, there is something for everyone in the family, not just women. Mary Holle started the store in 1985 with her sister. "I opened the store when I was around twenty-two, but it was much easier to open a store in that time. I loved antiques—jewelry, furniture, lighting, and lamps—and my sister loved antique clothing. I was also a natural buyer and seller. You can say it was in my blood."

The sisters decided to merge their passions. Back in the eighties, it was easier to procure products and there was simply just more to go around. Most of their items came from thrift stores and garage sales, and they still heavily rely upon consignments and estates sales. They opened the store with the findings from a princess's estate sale on Miami Beach. "It was such great stuff. We opened with racks and racks of twenties gowns, just gorgeous, one-of-a-kind, luxurious items." The sisters' mother was also in the business. She owned an antiques store in Homestead, which she eventually closed to join forces with her daughters.

When Miami Twice originally opened, they were situated among their peers, with at least four other vintage stores nearby. Located on Bird Road, between 57th and 67th Avenues, the area was previously known as Miami's Antique District. These days, the area is still a haven for fashionistas, but now it is filled with rows of modern boutiques. Back issues of *LIFE* and *People* magazines featuring the faces of Truman Capote, Liz Taylor, Frank Sinatra, and seventies Woody Allen and John Travolta; Chanel, Valentino, and Louis Vuitton handbags; fifties-inspired dresses and eighties jumpsuits; Jimmy Choos and Vera Wang; thirties Japanese Moriage Lithophane Dragon Tea Sets; knick-knacks and tchotchkes; masks; lamps; figurines; books; sunglasses; clothing; jewelry; and cameras are but the tip of the iceberg. Every inch of the large store features one-of-a-kind products, but the abundance of inventory is never overwhelming. The items are displayed in their best environment and with a designer's touch atop intricate vintage tables, armoires, and clothing racks. Even vintage earrings, which sell for as low as $5, are in impeccable condition, showing no defects and individually wrapped to preserve their quality. The front of the store features racks of new products, while the back is a vintage paradise ranging from the 1890s to the 1970s.

"We started as pure vintage, and ten years in we began incorporating new and non-vintage items," says Holle. "Fifteen years in, we began doing vintage costuming. Halloween is so big that the entire inventory is purchased by the first week of April." The incorporation of new and non-vintage items was a difficult decision, but a necessary one. eBay and general online shopping changed the way vintage is purchased around the world. "Miami is a nouveau riche city and as the years progressed, it has become harder and harder to procure vintage items," Holle says.

"As for mixing business and family, it has been just us since the beginning," she continues. "We are honest people and employ awesome people that are like family." One such employee has been around for eighteen years. "We have not been sucked into the consumerist lavishness that Miami is known for; we live within our means and that is just one of the many reasons we are still around."

MOLINA'S RANCH RESTAURANT

4090 E. EIGHTH AVE. • HIALEAH, FL 33013

(305) 693-4440 • MOLINASRANCHRESTAURANT.COM

Cuban Soul Food Palace

*E*veryone know Versailles, La Carreta, and Sergio's, but for a bit of old-school Cuban that is off the beaten path, folks head to Molina's Restaurant in Hialeah. While Versailles Disneyfied the notion of the Cuban restaurant, Molina's stuck to the simple roots of the culture.

Disclaimer: Do not go to Molina's hoping to find a ranch; this is just a good, old-fashioned Cuban spot housed in the Mediterranean architectural style that is common in most parts of Latin America. Some also say that the "Ranch" in the restaurant's name is a nod to the Cuban past as well as a nod to the area's historic past. Long before the Cubans in the sixties, the GIs in the forties and fifties, and even Hialeah Park, "The City of Progress" began as a sleepy dairy and farming town.

As I stated in my introduction, the establishments highlighted in these pages are sometimes more significant for the ethnic experience they provide than for their vintage appeal. Vintage in this example is more representative of another location. By Miami's standards, however, Molina's has stood the test of time. Originally opened in 1982 by Adolfo Molina, the current location is not the original. Over the decades the restaurant expanded from 83 to 203 seats due to its great popularity. And this has not kept the crowds away—there are regulars that have patronized the restaurant since the day it opened and they sit at the same tables, some even daily. The expansion has allowed for a larger watering hole atmosphere, as it now serves breakfast, along with the stalwart lunch and dinner. In the Latin community,

breakfast and the ever-famous *cafecito* are always the missing link to a great establishment.

A review of the restaurant in 1990 from the *Miami Herald* sums it up perfectly: "There are zillions of inexpensive Cuban restaurants in Miami. Most of them have a warm word and something edible to offer, even if it is just a sandwich and a jolt of coffee. The Cuban restaurant is one of Miami's real comforts of home, a warm and reliable way station in an otherwise icy world. It's more than a place to eat. It's one of life's constants. No matter which Cuban restaurant you choose, there's a thematic similarity to them, and it's generally satisfying. How many other American cities have a whole genre of restaurants that invite you to mosey in, put up your feet and loll amid a distinctly European sense of laissez-faire? It's to Molina's credit that it has put itself near the culinary forefront of the pack."

They serve all the classics, just like mamá: *pan con bistec, lechon asado, vaca frita, boliche asado,* Elena Ruth (while a traditional Cuban dish, it is rarely found on local menus), *chicharron de pollo* (or opt for regular pork *chicharrones*), ubiquitous black beans and rice, *gallina rellena* (stuffed Cornish hen), *mariquitas,* and for dessert, flan and *arroz con leche.* Wash it all down with a *batido* in flavors from papaya to wheat. One crazy standout is the *frituras de seso* (pig brains).

Another great nod to nostalgia and the concept of another culture and place is the way the restaurant looks and acts. Molina's is sparkling clean, spic-and-span, just like in a Cuban mother's home. The servers are not exactly fluent in English, so come armed with Spanish phrases or just go along for the ride of pointing. The worst that could happen is that you end up with the aforementioned pork brains. The servers, while lacking in language, make up for it with the preciseness of a synchronized swimmer clad in a red vest. The interior is like other Cuban restaurants: simple, with a lot of dark wood panel detailing in a cafeteria-like setting where the Cuban bread always arrives warm and toasty in red plastic bins.

Vintage Spot
VERSAILLES RESTAURANT: EST. 1971

Located on Calle Ocho on the perimeter of Little Havana, Versailles tags itself "The World's Most Famous Cuban Restaurant." The three-building complex offers something for everyone, with a full-service restaurant, a to-go window, and a bakery. If you want to learn about Cuban politics, make sure to stop in here.

3555 SW Eighth St.; (305) 444-0240; versaillesrestaurant.com

In the sea of tourism, which sometimes overruns Miami, it is nice to still find authentic places that are enjoyed as much by the locals as by the tourists. Local writers love to visit this spot, and even though it has been reviewed and rediscovered time and time again, it remains an untarnished gem. In 2005 the *Miami Herald* revisited the restaurant and recalled schoolboy memories of the current owner, who continues the legacy of Molina's today: "'I still remember being a cook here when I was 21 and loving every minute of it,' said owner José Orlando, 45, as he greets an elderly couple waiting to be seated. 'I was head chef for 13 years, and 11 years ago I bought the place from Adolfo Molina, who founded Molina's here in 1982. I follow his example every day and, just like he used to do, I spend most of my time here with the customers, many of them who know me since I was a kid trying to gather up a paycheck cooking their meals in the back.'"

MONTY'S RAW BAR

2550 S. BAYSHORE DR. • COCONUT GROVE, FL 33146

(305) 856-3992

Gilligan's Island in Miami

When you think of Miami, it would be hard to overlook Coconut Grove's iconic Monty's," says local Aubrey Swanson. "The raw bar was ingrained in my brain since the first day I moved down to Miami in 2006 to attend the University of Miami. It was the university's unofficial Friday-night happy hour hangout. And who could resist half-priced drinks from 4 p.m. to 8 p.m., live music, tiki hut ambience, and incredible bayside views? Oh yeah, and their famous potent drinks, the Pain Removers! Not to mention its close proximity to campus. In college, it was our go-to spot to kill the pain after the week's exams, projects, and lectures. It was the almost-guaranteed place to socialize with your college crush or dread seeing your ex; luckily there are multiple bars and lots of liquor at the restaurant. It was also the must-visit destination to take out-of-town visitors.

"After four years at the University of Miami, I figured I would not pay Monty's a visit nearly as frequently as I had in college, but boy was I wrong. Post-college, I entered the 'real world' and worked just two blocks away from the raw bar. It ended up being our go-to, post-work happy hour spot even on non-Friday nights. So to say I have spent a little bit of time at Monty's during my now eight years of living here in Miami would be an understatement. Whether you are a born-and-raised Miamian, college student, Miami transplant, or out-of-town visitor, you can bet Monty's has played a role in everyone's Miami experiences."

You may not find Ginger, Mary Ann, or the Professor, but come early and you will easily find your way into a chair, a tropical cocktail

or two, a variety of seafood such as peel-and-eat shrimp, dollar oysters, medium stone crabs when in season, conch fritters, and mahi mahi, along with an unobstructed view of Biscayne Bay on a huge outdoor deck shaded by thatched roof. On most nights, live reggae calypso music is played during happy hour. About those aforementioned Pain Removers, the menu explains it best: "Just Tell Us Where It Hurts! A Blend of Virgin Island Dark Rum, Cream of Coconut, Pineapple & Orange Juices, Served on the Rocks. Depending on How Much Pain You Are In, The Numbers 1, 2, & 3 Determine the Amount of Rum! Not Your Mother's Our!"

There is no need to drive to Key West or even Key Largo—a taste of the tropical life can be found right here in the heart of Coconut Grove. This bar has a loyal and devoted following, and since there are not many places like Monty's left, this is a one-of-a-kind treasure. It is easy to paint a picturesque scene of Monty's. As one of Miami's oldest bars, it takes patrons back to the days when Coconut Grove was still a pioneer village and Miami was a laid-back resort town. As Miami's first village, Bahamians and Americans unofficially established Coconut Grove in 1825 and operated it as an extension of the Bahamas until 1925. The history books note that the Bahamians lived a simple lifestyle, very much in tune with the land.

At the height of *Miami Vice* days, Michael Talbott, who played Detective Stan Switek, was a regular, and because of its low-key atmosphere, I would not be surprised if many more celebrities were regulars when visiting Miami. Remember the film *Marley & Me*? The scene where Marley, John, and Sebastian have lunch takes place at Monty's Raw Bar. The television series *Burn Notice*, when it was in production, also used the bar as a location.

While the original owner, Monty Trainer, sold his interest in 1986, his mission and soul continues to this day. They have now expanded to locations in Miami Beach, Key West, and Boca Raton, but this is where it all began. Now president of the Coconut Grove Arts & Historical Association, Trainer has been a longtime pioneer of the city. Along with Ted Arison, founder of Carnival Cruise Lines, he bid to bring the Miss Universe and Miss USA beauty pageants to Miami in 1982. They strongly believed that events of that caliber would help to change the city's image, which was tarnished and considered dangerous.

Trainer would go on to add to the negative stigma later in the decade, when he was sentenced to six months in prison and 25,000 hours of community service for tax evasion, but that is all in the past. In 2013 the *South Florida Business Journal* honored him with the Miami Ultimate CEO award. In an article by the same magazine, it is noted that "Trainer still considers Monty's Restaurant his greatest accomplishment and lasting legacy."

PINECREST WAYSIDE MARKET

10070 SW 57TH AVE. • MIAMI, FL 33165

(305) 661-6717

Home of the Famous Strawberry Shakes

A wayside market is one that is on the side of the road, way, path, or highway. This unassuming country-style shack, which sells produce, homemade salads and sandwiches, fresh bread and pastries, and juices, smoothies, and shakes, is located in the heart of Miami's garden village of Pinecrest.

Your eyes will instantly light up at the sight of the sprawling bright produce, very local and very fresh. Your sweet tooth will drool over local artisan treats such as Om Nom Nom cookies, Knaus Berry Farm cinnamon rolls, and their famous strawberry shakes. And finally, your inner foodie will fawn over homemade hummus, guacamole, salads, and sandwiches.

While the store has been around since 1948, it has changed owners four or five times. Eli Tako is the most recent owner, having purchased it in 2000. Here's an interesting and little-known fact: William and Evelyn Hirni, the original owners of the country store, also owned next-door neighbor Hirni's Wayside Garden Florist. They have gone on to pass, but their daughter, Janice, is still there. The friendly neighbors still hand-pollinate the giant sausage trees that hang out in front of the fruit shack.

A Miami native, Eli Tako grew up not too far from the store and was even a customer. Burnt out from the fashion industry, he took a leap of faith and purchased the property when it went up for sale. He wanted to be in a more laid-back atmosphere where he could be surrounded by food and families. And while it is not as laid-back as one would think, working around the clock and doing it all, from stocking

shelves to ringing up customers, he says it is a welcome departure from his previous life. He has maintained the store pretty much the same since its purchase.

Pinecrest Village is a tight-knit community, one that has roots in agriculture and, of course, gardens, as it is the home of the famed Fairchild Tropical Botanic Garden. In 1948 Pinecrest Wayside Market was a simple corner fruit stand on a dirt road surrounded by mangroves and avocados. The amount of mangos that grew in the area was so great that the shop also operated as a mango shipper. An old photo of the establishment during that time shows the horse and buggy as the main mode of transportation.

The village grew up and eventually became the ever-popular residential community that it is today, clad with lavish Mediterranean-style homes. The market is located on historic Red Road, which leads to Matheson Hammocks and Fairchild Garden. Not only does it offer a great country-style store for locals, who can get their provisions without having to trek to US 1, but it also makes a pleasant afternoon pit stop along the winding canal and mangrove-lined bike trails.

Tako makes sure to accommodate the locals, as they are his bread-and-butter. When he purchased the business, he kept the flash card file in place, an old-school system similar to memberships cards that was created by a previous owner. It is a client account system held inside of a flash card filer, where customers can rack up charges and then pay one lump sum at the end of the month, a concept that is long gone in all of Miami's stores. His prices are reasonable as well, which keeps the loyal customers coming back again and again. By picking up the products in Homestead himself every Wednesday, he cuts the costs of the middleman. His tomatoes sell for $1.39 a pound, as opposed to $1.59 or $1.89 a pound elsewhere.

Plus, Tako is great with the local producers and artisans, providing opportunities to the little guy as well. Chef Cristy's Raw Foods is one such little guy that has made it big in the community. She came to Tako a few years back with her products that are all raw, gluten free, no sodium, no cholesterol, and organic. He was initially hesitant to carry her velvet rolls and cinnamon rolls because of the higher price tag ($7.89 for a box of three rolls), but gave it a shot. Now, her products are Tako's most popular items, selling out almost immediately.

Another success that is a testament of great partnerships and community upbringing is that of Roc Kat, a local ice cream maker. The team behind Roc Kat is even purchasing an ice cream cooler for Tako so he can stock all of their flavors in his market.

The shack's most famous products are the shakes made with low-fat yogurt and real fruit, no additional sugar added. At only 90

Vintage Spot

ROBERT IS HERE: EST. 1959

This is Miami's charming country store and a frequent stop for travelers on the way to the Florida Keys. The open-air market is open November through August and the main draws are the unique shakes, made fresh from the area's bounty of mamey, pineapple, mango, and guava as well as the local honey. Fruit availability varies by season.

19200 SW 344th St.; (305) 246-1592; robertishere.com

calories, the shakes are a great way to "cheat" on your diet. Tako's favorite flavors are strawberry and espresso. He says the kids are usually partial to the Elvis and cookies and cream.

The always-smiling Tako is one of the most passionate folks you'll ever meet. "I grew up in this community and I want to continue the legacy that began in 1948. I know almost everyone that walks in and you know what? I love that. The kids I used to serve when I first started are now all grown up and still customers. The only difference is that now they drive themselves." Drive, bike, or walk to visit Eli Tako—his energetic vigor will brighten anyone's day.

THE RALEIGH HOTEL

1775 COLLINS AVE. • MIAMI BEACH, FL 33139

(305) 534-6300 • RALEIGHHOTEL.COM

Grand Dame of South Beach Art Deco

*L*ocated on Miami Beach's "hotel row" of Collins Avenue, both the avenue and the hotel offer a glimpse into the past. This special tour of the past begins at the Carlton South Beach Hotel a few streets down on 14th. Begin the trek on Collins Avenue, and you will immediately see traces of the past with Jerry's Famous Deli and old hotel signs like the Royal Palm, The Ritz, and diLido. The northeast corner of Lincoln Road and Collins Avenue is the former home of the famous Wolfie's Restaurant; sadly now only memories of the sky-high sandwiches remain.

Continue walking, and you will pass more iconic hotels like the National, the Delano, and the South Seas before reaching the final destination of the Raleigh, offering an air of exclusivity behind its intricate and lush landscaping that transports guests to the era of the forties. With its royal blue Art Deco signage, terrazzo floors, cedar wood pieces, and nautical awnings and umbrellas, seventy-four years after its opening, the hotel remains timeless and as luxurious and chic as ever.

Opened in 1940, the Raleigh was built by architect L. Murray Dixon. As one of the principal architects of the Art Deco South Beach style, he is also credited with such iconic hotels as the Ritz Plaza and The Tides, which is located on Ocean Drive. From the Shore Corporation to Brilla Group to Sam Nazarian and SBE, the hotel has had many owners and various renovations, but none have removed its charm and beauty. In April 2014 Tommy Hilfiger paid $56.5 million for the Raleigh. Preservationists and locals alike remain hopeful that its history will not be demolished.

Originally farmland, Miami Beach exploded as a beachfront community in the twenties, with much of its Art Deco and Art Moderne architecture to follow in the thirties and forties (over forty hotels were built between 1940 and 1942 alone). The hotel opened to lavish festivities on New Year's Eve 1940, and during the opening, a local then-unknown drummer named Desi Arnaz replaced a sick band member. The hotel has not always been a hotel, though: In times of war, like all other hotels in the area, it was used to house soldiers. After World War II, the forties were a boom era for much of Miami Beach, and in contrast to the nearby Clay Hotel, which is not located oceanfront, the Raleigh was extremely popular.

On its seventy-year anniversary in 2010, I had the pleasure of interviewing a gentleman in his late eighties who honeymooned at the Raleigh with his young bride shortly after it opened. As part of the celebratory initiatives, the couple was invited back to the hotel to stay in the same suite. The most memorable part of the interview is when he rejoiced that there would be air-conditioning this time around.

The management noted that at one point the Raleigh was even a kosher hotel. Other amenities once included dance classes and a card room. According to a story that appeared in the *Daytona Beach Morning Journal* on March 1, 1982, during Prohibition it was common for hotels to have the aforementioned card rooms, which hosted illegal gambling. Fashionable with the senior citizens, they played penny ante poker, but when the cops busted in, they did not want to arrest old people, so it was a bust gone bad.

The hotel's most iconic feature is the lovely but oddly shaped pool, made famous by actress and swimmer Esther Williams. *LIFE* magazine also named it the most beautiful pool in America. For the younger crowd, the pool is featured as a backdrop in the popular nineties movie *The Birdcage*. Surrounded by various wading pools, fountains, and palm fronds, it is a tropical oasis in the heart of South Beach. Its odd shape has made it famous the world over, leaving many stumped as to how to label it or even describe it. Is it a crest, a fleur-de-lis, a Rorschach blot? The answer remains unknown.

The Raleigh Hotel was Esther Williams's favorite place to stay on visits to Miami Beach in the fifties, and the hotel honors her loyalty with a suite in her name. "The Esther Williams Suite is named after the Hollywood star of the same name," says hotel concierge Fernando

Montealegre. "She was an actress of worldwide appeal and fame. She was known primarily for movies where she showed off her swimming skills and that showcased big Hollywood-set-style aquatic sequences such as *Poseidon's Daughter* and *Million Dollar Mermaid*. The suite is named after her because it is grand, occupying the entire eastern wing of the seventh floor, and because it faces the ocean and pool. It consists of a huge parlor and living room and a bedroom portion."

In terms of food, Blue Star Restaurant was short-lived but all the rage; led by Kerry Simon in the nineties, it drew an A-list crowd. After he departed to open Starfish and later build his fame in other states, the hotel's restaurants have not been as successful. In 2003 Eric Ripert of the famous Le Bernardin did a stint at the hotel as cuisine director. But not until 2013, with the introduction of Restaurant Michael Schwartz, has the hotel enjoyed such foodie acclaim. "I always said the only way I would ever do something in South Beach would be to do something there," says chef and local restaurateur Michael Schwartz. "There, being the Raleigh, an iconic property."

One final note: At the very least, stop in for a cocktail at the Martini Bar or just check out the pool.

ROYAL CASTLE

2700 NW 79TH ST. • MIAMI, FL 33147

(305) 696-8241

James Brimberry's Royal Castle

*A*t the height of the company's popularity, Royal Castles were as abundant as modern-day McDonald's, with hundreds of outposts across the South Florida region. Best known for their famous tagline "Fit For a King" (this slogan was built into the terrazzo floors of all outlets), there is an infinite number of stories and memories surrounding the former fast-food king.

An ad from the forties stated that more than 3 million Royal Castle hamburgers were sold annually in Miami. The restaurants were especially popular during wartime for their affordable prices. Those who grew up when Royal Castles proliferated lament them greatly. Most nostalgia stems from the tasty burgers themselves or their signature birch beer, another cult classic. A 1962 article from the *Miami News* noted that Royal Castle produced its birch beer in bottles for local supermarkets, for those that needed easy access to the libation at all times.

Its exterior design is so iconic that you can still spot converted Royal Castles all around the county. The restaurant is rectangular in shape, while its roof protrudes past the building's base on all sides like a fancy rectangular hat. Clad in all white, the orange namesake bubble letters stand out, along with the cheerful logo of a boy with a crown holding a burger. Ten silver stools stand at the red-and-white counter. A sixties-era poster for Coca-Cola hangs on the wall. Other locations in Miami included 87th Avenue and Bird Road, 202 W. Flagler St., and 132 NE Second Ave.

Probably the most unique promotional piece was the 1967 Miami Dolphins cards issued by Royal Castle restaurants strictly in the Miami

area. Printed on thin cardboard, there were twenty-eight cards in a set. The cards, even when originally distributed, were rare and valuable; the top card was that of Bob Griese. Two cards were made available each week of the 1967 football season.

Royal Castle was Miami's first foray into fast food, founded in 1938 by William Singer; the restaurants were modeled after another hamburger icon, White Castle. The economic state of the country during the Great Depression and afterwards during the war led to an increased popularity in fast-food restaurants. Dwindling from the hundreds, only two Royal Castle locations with different owners still exist, and both restaurants are located a mere ten minutes from each other. The only change James Brimberry has made to the classic menu at his 79th Street location over the decades is to add "country food": grits, runny eggs, pork chops, ham. Not surprisingly, the best seller is the $10.99 T-bone steak.

Wayne Arnold owns the location at 12490 NW Seventh Ave. He was let go after the company went out of business in 1976, but eventually purchased one of the last remnants of the empire in 1980. In the middle of 2014, the iconic restaurant was converted into Finga Licking @ Royal Castle, a restaurant serving a mix of Caribbean food and soul food. Now, the shell and the ode to the name are the only remnants of the once-great Royal Castle on that block. They even tore out the beautiful terrazzo floors.

But, let us not forget that this is the story of James Brimberry and his Royal Castle! Who is he anyway? Originally from Liberty City, Brimberry owns the location at 2700 NW 79th St. Royal Castle restaurants were in full operation during the civil rights movements of the sixties but did not allow black customers to sit at the counter, instead forcing them to order items through a side window. It was a hotbed of discrimination, not only for blacks, but for women as well. After the Civil Rights Act of 1964, Brimberry was hired as the first black manager for the brand.

A *Miami Herald* article from 2008 highlighting local businesses and their history perfectly recalls the struggles the restaurant faced after integration: "Being from the military, they knew that I would be able to withhold animosity and my tongue and my anger, and deal with some of the things that would be thrown in front of me," Brimberry is quoted as saying. The white folks at the time were not happy and made it difficult for Brimberry, but he persevered. He said to himself: "One day, I am going to own this company."

In 1976 his dreams became a reality after the company left eight stores to Brimberry. Over time he sold seven stores and even owned the Finga Licking location before it burned down in 2005. After the big changeover at the 125th Street location, James Brimberry's Royal Castle is now officially the last vestige of a now-defunct empire. Today, the restaurant is a nostalgic nod to the past in flavor and design, where the old customs of racism are thankfully long gone and where the burgers are still cheap.

S&S DINER

1757 NE SECOND AVE. • MIAMI, FL 33132

(305) 373-4291

Miami's Greasy Spoon

Jf a restaurant is on Anthony Bourdain's itinerary, it is bound to be good. He visited S&S Diner on the Miami episode of *The Layover* a few years back, to eat meat loaf with grits and gravy and peas. He called the iconic diner a Twilight Zone. Indeed, it is an old-school greasy spoon in the neighborhood of Edgewater, just north of the Central Business District of downtown Miami.

After Tobacco Road and Mac's Club Deuce, S&S Diner is Miami's oldest-running establishment, and it has not changed much since Mr. and Mrs. A. G. Sease (their first names are unknown) opened it in the summer of 1938, a time when the entire country was dealing with the Great Depression and cheap meals were essential. This combined with their unpretentious environment and on-the-go eating made diners especially popular and essential during the thirties. If that is not enough history for you, it is also located directly across from the City of Miami Cemetery, where Julia Tuttle, William Burdine, and Dr. James Jackson are buried.

Just a stone's throw from Biscayne Boulevard, S&S has remained strong through decades of immense change in the area. Before the Wynwood boom in the early 2000s and even the Omni boom in the eighties, this diner stood alone, but the people still came. Built in the forties and fifties as an alternative getaway to the expensive and gauche Miami Beach, Biscayne Boulevard is lined with old motels between 50th and 77th Streets. Though the area had been built up after World War II, people began to move out, and by the eighties Biscayne Boulevard consisted of mostly rundown motels, prostitutes,

and high crime rates. From seedy to trendy, in a *Miami Herald* article from April 16, 2014, the city's most notable historian, Paul George, said the transformation has been fascinating to watch: "It is a fabulous story of urban revival."

So, what's on the menu? A lot of eggs, a lot of high-stacked pancakes, and the 2-2-2-2 special is a must—two pancakes, two eggs, two pieces of bacon, and two sausage patties. Waitresses take an order and shout it to the cooks through a little window. Every Tuesday is Thanksgiving at the diner, offering all the trimmings of a proper holiday dinner with turkey, mashed potatoes, gravy, and cranberry. It is usually a busy night.

In 1989 S&S was added to the National Register of Historic Places. The official report, produced by City of Miami preservation officers Ellen Uguccioni and Sara E. Eaton, states that S&S is a designated establishment because it is an example of the Art Deco style through its design, ornamentation, materials, and use of pigmented structural glass and aluminum: "The diner employs a three-color scheme of beige, white and red to create the geometric banding on the wall surface and porthole windows." In the restaurant's case, S&S "is Miami's only known remaining example of the type of small restaurant that was popular throughout the United States during the thirties. Diners and sandwich shops were once a common building type, but most of these have disappeared."

S&S sports a typical diner atmosphere inside and out. A large chef statue welcomes guests to the tiny beige-and-white building flanked by red awnings. Once inside, the U-shaped counter lined with red leather stools is the diner's centerpiece. The menus are laminated and serve as placemats as well. Walls are lined with movie posters, awards, and old photos. Free parking is available in the alley behind the diner. Most surprising in our credit-card-crazed society, it remains a cash-only establishment after seventy-plus years. This is the type of place where they call you hon and sweetie, where your coffee mug is never empty, and where the median age of the staff is around fifty.

In 2011 S&S Diner expanded with a second location inside of Allen's Drug Store, another entry in this book, replacing Picnics Restaurant. The diner went into preservation mode, protecting itself in case it was booted out of its home. Miami was and is in boom mode, and the diner is located in a prime spot for high-rises, similar to the story of Tobacco Road. After much negotiating, the restaurant's location remains safe. Eventually current owner Charles Cavalaris reliquished ownership of the second location. The two S&S locations now only share a name.

In 2013, for the first time, the diner opened its doors past regular dining hours for special events. One such event called Diner & A Movie was a two-seating and two-screening affair "merging passions that we love like eating at our local haunts; catching a great film at an art house; or just getting out and discovering new facets of this city we call home. Miami is getting more lovable by the day!" In the kitchen was Amanda Fischer of Ruthie's and Suzanne Barr of It's Always Home. The fifties-diner-inspired New Orleans–style cuisine was paired with the classic film *A Streetcar Named Desire*.

Who does not love a good old-fashioned greasy spoon? In Miami where IHOPs and Denny's abound, S&S Diner offers a breath of old air and fits the bill for those with a hankering for comfort food. "We never change, and the fact that we never change is why people like us," says Elfi Robinson, longtime waitress, in a 2013 article on *Eater.*

SEDANO'S SUPERMARKET

VARIOUS LOCATIONS THROUGHOUT MIAMI

SEDANOS.COM

¡Sigue la Tradición!

ell, I like Sedano's Supermarket for a number of reasons," says local food enthusiast Marvin Tapia. "First, they carry a lot of original Central and South American brands that remind us Hispanics of our home countries. Second, they play bachata and salsa music while you shop. Finally, most locations have cafeterias, which I like to visit for a pre- or post-shopping *cafecito, pastelito,* and/or *croqueta.* If these things do not scream 'Only in Miami,' then I do not know what does. The Sedano's I visit is the one in Miami Lakes, close to my parents' home. The ladies at the cafeteria already know me, and I go every time I visit my parents."

Simply referred to as Sedano's, it is one of the top supermarkets in Miami, alongside Publix and Winn-Dixie, and the first of its kind in the city. Nationwide, it is the top Hispanic retailer in the United States, and it only has locations in Florida.

The old-fashioned meat department is just one of the reasons Sedano's is popular. It sells pork in a variety of forms from cube size to whole raw pigs, popular during the holiday seasons, when Cubans roast pigs in Caja Chinas in their backyard. The entire store is just fun to shop in; they stock items that residents outside of South Florida have little knowledge about, and it is not only commercialized products like Bustelo, Goya, and Pilon, but products like Harina PAN, Nuestra Familia, Ramona's, San Marcos, La Preferida, Nido, Herdez, Dolores Tuna, Charras, La Sierra, Gilda, Arrachera, La Chona, Emperador and V&V Supremo.

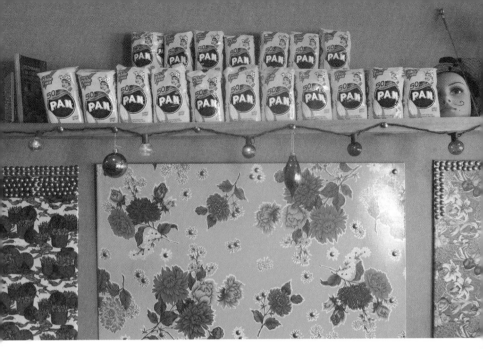

They also sell recognizable products like Mott's and Hershey's, but then you will stumble upon items like Paleton de Cajeta (Mexican goat milk lollipops) and Panelitas de Arequipe y Coco (milk caramel with coconut, a typical sweet in the Caribbean nations). The brand El Guapo easily replaces Badia. The frozen foods section is extra special, with brands like El Sembrador and La Fe. The checkout lanes are smaller, similar to the home country, and feature *Vanidades* magazine and tamarind balls instead of *Cosmopolitan* and M&Ms.

Sedano's also has a great hot food bar, selling items like shredded beef, *chicharrones*, rice and beans, and tamales. And at the previously mentioned in-store cafeterias, you can buy a variety of delicious pastries by the item or the pound. Additionally, there are usually ethnic food carts outside the stores selling items like arepas and churros. Essentially, this is where you go for your introduction to Latin foods, and food lovers can easily spend hours studying new ingredients and brands. It is common for the employees to greet you in Spanish.

A typical conversation that can be heard at any store: "I live on Eighth and Nineteenth, it's a different life here. My kids behave, but have you seen the kid on that block? He's disrespectful. If I had done that in my time, it would've been something else. *Eso no pasaba en*

Cuba, chica." Translation: "Girl, that never happened in Cuba." It is a common phrase.

Founded by Rene Sedano in 1961, he quickly sold the store to Armando Guerra in 1962. Like most businesses in Miami, this one has its roots in Cuba. In 1971 Guerra brought on Manuel Herran to help with the daily operations. It remains a family business, with Herran's son at the helm. Herran married into the Guerra family and was the main catalyst behind the rapid expansion of the supermarket. Interestingly enough, most of the stores are incorporated separately and owned by other family members who manage the store. The first store is called Hialeah #1 and is located at 840 E. 41st Street in Hialeah. There are now thirty-four supermarkets in the portfolio.

In 1986 a frenzy occurred at a local Sedano's parking lot. The *Miami News* story from June 30 reported, "About 30 people gathered in the parking lot of the Sedano's Supermarket at Palm Avenue and West 39th Street, watching the lights with growing concern and repeatedly calling police from pay phones outside the store. Alas, there is an earthly explanation—a trailer with four small but high intensity white search lights in the lot of Colonial Pontiac were left on during the night, and the rotating beams danced across the clouds over South Florida." Everyone thought they were UFOs.

Another interesting event occurred on Cinco de Mayo in 2013, when a mariachi band serenaded customers at a store. Sedano's is very involved in the community, participating in local events such as The Miami-Dade County Fair and the Three Kings Parade on Calle Ocho. What has also made the store successful is that it caters to the specific neighborhood in which it is located. But that does not mean they are not getting competition from the other leaders of the pack; Publix has a line of supermarkets called Publix Sabor, which are more Hispanic influenced.

Like their tagline says, *¡Sigue la tradición!* Sedano's continue the tradition of the old country in the new without skipping a beat. As an individual that frequents many a supermarket abroad, I can attest to this fact.

SEYBOLD JEWELRY BUILDING

36 NE FIRST ST. • MIAMI, FL 33132

(305) 374-7922 • SEYBOLDJEWELRY.COM

Glittering Miami

*A*ll that glitters is not just gold, but diamonds, gems, silver, and pearls—all the things that make women's hearts pit-ter-patter. Located in the heart of downtown Miami, the Seybold Building offers a special, one-of-a-kind experience for shop-pers looking to add an extra bit of glitz and bling to their life. As the second-largest jewelry building in the United States, behind Los Ange-les' Jewelry Trades Building, the Seybold Building serves as the anchor for Miami's Jewelry District, which spans four city blocks from Miami Avenue to SE Second Avenue on Flagler Street and NE First Street.

With its interior fluorescent lighting and neon signage, the Seybold Building feels like a building comprised of duty-free shops, but it is actually up to New York's prestigious Fifth Avenue standards. Officially on the National Register of Historic Places, the arcade-style building houses over 280 jewelers on ten floors. Tenants include such jewelers as Albert's Fine Jewelers, Nemaro Jewelers, Dasani Jewels, Freddy's Jewelry, and Buchwald Jewelers, which is the building's oldest tenant, open since 1932. Shareef Malnik, local owner of the Forge Restaurant (also a vintage establishment highlighted in the pages of this book), boasts that he is a longtime customer of Buchwald Jewelers on his blog, his staple purchases being the upscale watches.

This is not the kind of place you go in to leisurely walk around—you go in with a mission and a plan. A little-known fact, many of Miami's most eligible bachelors purchase their engagement rings here before going off the market. This is also ground zero for the international jewelry trade, and many Miami-based distributor supply stores in St. Maarten, the US Virgin Islands, Puerto Rico, the Dominican Republic, Aruba, Mexico, and Central and South America.

John Seybold was one of the first passengers on the Florida East Coast Railway on its newest stop at Miami. He did not know it at the time, but the German-born immigrant would become one of the most important settlers to the area. Shortly after his arrival, he opened a lunch counter on Miami's first street, Avenue D. Local entrepreneur L. F. Hoefer also operated a bakeshop on the site of what is now the Seybold Building. Eventually, Seybold began working with him, delivering bread to the many households around town via horse and wagon. In 1915 Seybold bought Hoefer out and added a lunchroom and ice cream parlor to the bakery, renaming the building after himself. Since Julia Tuttle did not permit saloons in Miami, Seybold's ice cream parlor became the social center of the young city. Known as the Mother of Miami, Tuttle's master persuasion led Henry Flagler to extend his Florida East Coast Railway all the way down to Miami. The city was subsequently built and incorporated on a large part of her donated land, with the condition that it would remain dry.

Skyscrapers sprouted all over downtown Miami during the boom era of the twenties, mainly in the architectural style of the Mediterranean Revival, thanks in part to architecture firm Kiehnel & Elliott. Stuccoed walls, red-tiled roofs, windows in the shape of arches,

wrought-iron balconies, rectangular floor plans, and symmetry are common benchmarks of the Mediterranean Revival style. Included on the list of important Mediterranean Revival–style buildings in Miami are the Carlyle Hotel in Miami Beach and the Coconut Grove Playhouse in Coconut Grove. In 1925 the Seybold Building expanded to encompass ten floors. With entrances on both Flagler and First Streets, the building has remained a center for fashionable shopping throughout its entire history.

Southern Bakeries eventually absorbed Seybold's baking operations. In 1932 he introduced a new loaf of bread called Southern Milk, and it was supplied to grocery stores around southeastern Florida. It was heralded as his most popular bread, as it conformed to the US government milk bread formula. On October 27, 1932, the *Palm Beach Post* tracked the impressive trajectory of one of Miami's foodie forefathers: "From the one-man bakery of pioneer days, it is now one of the largest plants in Florida. Whereas a horse and wagon are sufficient to deliver the plant's output in the nineties, now a large fleet of trucks makes rapid deliveries to the Greater Miami area and the East Coast of Florida. In 1924, John Seybold was elected president of the Southern Bakers' Association. John Seybold was the official seller of Elmer's Chocolates during the time his store was in operation."

"At the Seybold Building, it feels a bit like you have to be let in on a secret," says local fashion writer Patricia Guarch Wise on *Racked.* "Buchwald Jewelers is located on the first floor of the building in the arcade space, where it is lined in neon signs and security guards yelling at you if you try and take a picture—beware selfie takers and compulsive Instagrammers, it does not fly here. One store told me it is because some of the high-profile clientele do not want to be photographed, which is laughable, but I kind of like the anti-snapshot policy because it adds to the old-school feel."

SHORTY'S BAR-B-Q

9200 S. DIXIE HWY. • MIAMI, FL 33156
(305) 670-7732 • SHORTYS.COM

Shorty's Stands Tall against BBQ Competition

*R*ibs, chicken, slaw, pork, fried okra, sweet potatoes . . . Like any other barbecue place, Shorty's is not trendy or fancy, but it sure is an institution offering decent prices, abundant plates, and nostalgic comfort food. Even though Miami is geographically part of the South, authentic barbecue joints are few and far between. Lucky for Miamians, the city offers barbecue weather all year long, and the interest in such establishments has increased exponentially in the last few years.

In Miami, the original rise in the popularity of barbecue occurred in the forties and fifties, when good ole Americana tastes ruled the city. Over the course of Miami's history, there has always been a standby barbecue restaurant. Let us remember the ones that are no longer with us: Ole Hickory, Farrington's, and Bar-B-Que Barn. Interest in barbecue did not completely die off, but it was overshadowed by the new and foreign flavors of the Caribbean in the sixties. Barbecue made a comeback in the seventies, specifically with the trend of succulent ribs led by local restaurant empire Tony Roma's.

When some people say Shorty's, others holler out Shiver's, and vice versa. Barbecue wars in Miami are no joke. The recently resurfaced Uncle Tom's Barbecue, Pit BBQ, People's BBQ, Shiver's, and finally Shorty's are the last remaining beacons from the old days of Miami. More modern representations of barbecue are Sparky's Roadside Barbecue, Pride and Joy BBQ, and Brother Jimmy's BBQ.

Farther down US 1 you will find Shiver's, with only one outpost. When it first opened, it was practically the only restaurant on the road toward the Keys. There are different stories about the rivalry between Shorty's and Shiver's, but the correct one is that Shorty Allen and Virgil Shiver were business partners who split up to open separate restaurants with the same theme. Shiver beat Allen by one year.

Edward Louis Allen, more commonly known as Shorty, passed away at the great age of 104 in 2013. Originally from Georgia, he opened the iconic restaurant in 1951 on US 1 in the then-rural area of Pinecrest. The restaurant proved to be popular and expanded to two other locations, one on Bird Road and the other in Broward. He sold the restaurant in the eighties. Mark Vasturo, the restaurant empire's current president and CEO, is no stranger to nostalgic establishments, as he previously worked for the late Rascal House.

Shorty's suffered a great fire in 1972 and burned to the ground, but it was rebuilt shortly thereafter. Prior to the location's burning, the smoke that came out of the pit was so thick that it would cloud drivers' vision on US 1. Ironically, a spark from the antipollution device installed to prevent such black smoke ignited the grease fire in the kitchen.

Shorty's is still a trip back in time, even though they have made modern upgrades. For decades the restaurant did not have air-conditioning and featured open windows and natural breezes. This is a country place through and through; there are no private tables, only communal dining seating across long wooden tables. Instead of napkins, rolls of paper towels are placed in the middle of tables to encourage further conviviality. Most of the food on the menu gets cooked at the giant grill complex. Like several other establishments in this book, many of the servers have been around for decades, some as long as thirty years.

It is said that the Pinecrest location serves up to 300 pounds of ribs a day. Heck, I believe it. Drive past the restaurant on any given day, and the parking lot is always full and folks crowd the entrance. Its smoky and sweet scent always entices me as I sit in traffic after a long workday. I am sure it has tempted many to forgo the gridlocked traffic of US 1 for an impromptu dinner.

A little known fact is that Shorty's serves Terry's Key Lime Pie, which is credited with helping make key lime pie the official pie of Florida. It was created by Bob Roth's New River Groves in Davie. The difference in the pie is that it comes with whipped topping instead of meringue.

One last tidbit of history: The Burger King located nearby is #6, meaning it is the sixth Burger King ever built. Sadly, it has lost its old-time feel over years of corporate brand changes.

When at Shorty's, do not neglect to get messy. If you are not getting messy, you are not doing it right! That is what the Wet-Naps and paper towels are for.

Vintage Spot

UNCLE TOM'S BARBECUE: EST. 1948

This is Miami's original finger-licking deliciousness. The restaurant has stood unassumingly on Eighth Street since the forties, but offers some of the best barbecue south of Atlanta. After temporarily shuttering its doors due to a dilapidating structure, Uncle Tom's is back at it with new digs in the same location, but it has not lost its signature good eats or its vintage feel.

3988 SW Eighth St.; (305) 445-0844; utbbq.com

STEPHEN'S RESTAURANT

1000 E. 16TH ST. • HIALEAH, FL 33010

(305) 887-8863 • STEPHENSOFHIALEAH.COM

The Last of the Gringos in Hialeah

grew up in the suburbs right outside of New York City, and even there in the mecca of Jewish delis, they do always get it right," says local writer Zachary Fagenson. "Being Jewish myself, I know my deli, and there is more to the craft than meets the eye. To find a place in Hialeah that does it right is completely mind blowing. At Stephen's, they get a whole brisket, cure it, and hand carve it. Although I live nowhere near it, I try to go as often as I can. Located in far reaches of Hialeah, in the heart of the mostly barren warehouse district, you really just have to know that it is there. But, I can see how it was a hot spot back in the day. These days, however, most businesses are located on the 49th Street retail corridor and of Cuban origin."

In the middle of Hialeah lies an area stuck in time, an abandoned warehouse district that houses not one, but two delis, Stephen's Restaurant and Franky's Deli Warehouse, prompting many to do a double take. This is the story of Stephen's, although no one really remembers who Stephen was or how the name came about. The restaurant is a reminder of a different time in Hialeah, when Glenn Curtiss and James Bright created the city as the entertainment center of Miami, with attractions such as Hialeah Park Race Track and Miami Jai-Alai.

In the fifties Hialeah's warehouse district became an important garment-manufacturing hub, and the rest of the city, home to a large Jewish population. Despite the area's rapidly changing demographics in the sixties, lines wrapped outside Stephen's doors, and this continued well into the seventies. As Miami's overall community changed, the garment industry moved out and with it, the Jewish population.

These days the area is largely a shipping and distribution hub, and most of Stephen's clientele come from these nearby establishments. An interesting note, Hialeah has the highest percentage of Cuban and Cuban-American residents of any city in the United States, at 74 percent of the population. A clash of various cultures and new populations drastically transformed the city into a working-class community. And while most of the Jewish population no longer resides in Hialeah, they still make the trek from all reaches of South Florida to eat at the historic restaurant.

Opened in 1954, original owners Sheldon and Phyllis Nadelman came from New York. Chef Henderson "Junior" Biggers has worked at Stephen's since it opened, and sixty years later, this is the only job he has had in Miami. The chef is as much of an icon as the restaurant. The centerpiece of the restaurant is not its deli ambience or even the people, but the homemade, hand-sliced pastrami and corned beef. Biggers has been quoted as saying that the key to perfect corned beef is not to overcook it. As Fagenson pointed out, everything at Stephen's is hand carved, with Biggers at the helm.

There have been various owners over the years, and since 2011 Jack Frisch has made Stephen's home. Not much has changed at the

restaurant since it opened. The biggest developments include the addition of salads and wraps to keep up with the times, and every now and then, there are off-the-menu specials.

As a traditional New York–style deli, Stephen's retains its old-timey feel, with wood-paneled walls, seventeen circular stools along a curved Formica-countertop bar, and old pictures along the wall. With their attention to quality and large portions, the food at Stephen's has been compared to that of the iconic Rascal House (RIP). Like many old-school places, this is still very much a boys' club. Some interesting tidbits: In the sixties, it was the official meeting place for the Southern Society of Paint Technology. For a modern reference, it is a favorite of local *Miami Herald* critic Victoria Pesce Elliott.

Owner Frisch, a former headhunter from New Jersey, did what others only dream of doing. He stuck it to the man, enrolled in the culinary program at nearby Johnson & Wales University, and became his own boss with the purchase of Stephen's Restaurant. And while he may not have decades of experience, he worked under renowned chef Michael Psilakis, formerly of Eos in the Viceroy Hotel. Like many who enter the culinary world, Frisch realized early on that the restaurant business does not generally offer favorable hours, and therefore narrowed his search to strictly breakfast and lunch spots. Now, he works thirteen-hour days instead of sixteen-hour days.

"The Reuben and the Rachel are iconic sandwiches. The restaurant does not do anything out of the ordinary, but it is different for Miami because there are not any other restaurants that make or sell the Rachel, and historically the Ruben and the Rachel are just typical Jewish names." The Rachel sandwich is a variation on the standard Reuben, substituting pastrami for corned beef and coleslaw for sauerkraut.

The local government wants to revitalize the stretch of street on which the deli is located into a neighborhood similar to the Wynwood Arts District, which also functioned as a garment district in the younger days of Miami. (More information about Wynwood can be found in the Austin Burke chapter.) Stephen's Restaurant serves as an example of a community that has dramatically changed over the decades, but still retains the culture of all who have passed through it. Plan to visit this and other Hialeah landmarks while in the area.

SUNSET CORNERS FINE WINE AND SPIRITS

8701 SW 72ND ST. • MIAMI, FL 33173
(305) 271-8492 • SUNSETCORNERS.COM

Mac Daddies of Wine

"And meandering through the Sunset Corners spirits shop I found what may be the biggest collection of wines this side of New York. Prime-year vintages of Pauillac, Margauz and St. Julien of the Bordeaux; a '49 Chateau Haut Brion (at $19.95!), Beaujolais, Rhone, Loire; scores of Burgundies, including the famed Chambertin, Vougeot, Vosne Romanee, Domaine de la Romance-Conti (a '61 La Tache at $13.95), and bargains in Puligny Montrachet plus a full list of Rheingau, Palatinate and Moselles from Germany. Including what may be the world's best wine—a '62 Eiswein, at $19.95 a bottle."

—goodies and calories in the *Miami News*,
October 23, 1965

From the above excerpt in the now-defunct *Miami News* to holding such accolades as the *Miami New Times*' Best Liquor Store and *Market Watch Magazine*'s Retailer of the Year, there is no doubt that Sunset Corners has been popular since it opened. Now in its sixtieth year, the store's legacy continues with the second generation of owners, Mike Bittel and Larry Solomon.

Bernie and Rosalind Rudnick, Bittel's and Solomon's grandparents, moved to Miami in the hopes that their daughter's illness would improve. In those days, Miami's naturally balmy climate was touted

for its healing powers. Before the acquisition of Sunset Corners, Bernie was a distillery rep for Glenmore Company, a producer of bourbon whiskey, and represented Florida and the Caribbean as their top dog. Hands changed and eventually the new owner who was anti-Semitic fired him, as was common at the time. From then on, he vowed to work for himself.

Shortly thereafter, in December 1954, the couple purchased a preexisting walk-up liquor store on the corner of Sunset Drive, when the area was still a rural farming community. An interesting and little known fact: The original liquor store still exists within Sunset Corners; the size of a large closet, it is now used as a storage space for products in the back of the house.

In the early 1960s the couple rebuilt the store, adding the Hex Bar and Lounge, a hexagonal bar that was named best bar in Miami to have an affair, because it was so dark. True to its descriptions, Bittel says that you could not even see the person in front of you. The bar featured a Scopitone machine, the only one in Miami. The predecessor to the music video, it is a jukebox that shows three minutes of living-color musical production film. The renovation also brought the addition of grocery carts, and they were the first liquor store in the area to do that. (They no longer provide grocery carts for shopping.)

In the 1980s a lucky accident set the stage for the vision of the business for years to come. A regular asked the owner to purchase a case of Château Haut-Brion. Instead, what arrived was its direct competitor with a similar name, La Mission Haut-Brion. The issue was quickly resolved, but the owners realized the new opportunities and profitability of the increasingly popular wine market. Prior to this, their inventory mainly focused on rum and whiskey, the brown kings of liquor. In 1983 came another renovation. The Hex Bar and Lounge sadly closed and customers could not get hexed in anonymity anymore, the deli was put in, and the store expanded.

These days wine sales make up about 60 percent of the company's overall sales. Interesting enough, most of their sales are done online, with the majority of orders coming from California. Their wines range in price from $5 to well over $2,000. Bittel is most proud of the quality of the cheaper selections they have on hand: "It's easy to stock the Châteauneuf-du-Papes of the world, but the $5 and $10 bottles of wine require a more knowledgeable palate to seek out the best. You can buy cheap wine anywhere these days. I dare you to find a place that puts as much effort into the lower-priced wines as they do their expensive ones."

The $7 Stemmari Nero d'Avola is Bittel's favorite and not coincidentally the store's top seller in wines. He further stresses that the three distinct qualities of price, service, and knowledge set them apart and that you have to have all of the ingredients to make it work.

"The world has changed quite a lot from the old rural farming days," Bittel says. "We now live in a city that is international, which makes our clientele diverse, keeping us on our toes, and I find that genuinely fascinating. We run our business as a dozen little stores within a store. Each section, whether it be beer, wine, or liquor, has its own manager, and they are the experts in that sector. With the advent of the Internet and better technology, we have to be one step ahead of everyone else in terms of knowledge." He half-jokingly notes that his favorite pastime is pairing wine with food.

A Miami company through and through, the partners make sure to stay active in the community, a way to keep the Sunset Corners legacy strong, running, and continually growing. They have an unofficial partnership with local Florida International University, with two positions at the store allotted to students who want to learn about

the industry. Sunset Corner "alums" have gone on to be successful wine entrepreneurs and sommeliers. The cousin-owners are also
founding members of VeritageMiami, previously the Miami Wine and
Food Festival, a popular charity event that spans five days and hosts
a variety of exciting seminars, social functions, and tastings.

TAP TAP RESTAURANT

819 FIFTH ST. • MIAMI BEACH, FL 33139

(305) 672-2898 • TAPTAPMIAMIBEACH.COM

Intro to Haitian Culture

Founded in 1994 by Katherine Kean, Haitians do not actually own the restaurant. Story is, Kean visited Haiti and fell in love with the culture, and she wanted to share it with the local community of Miami. Twenty years later, she is still providing the magic.

According to food writer and gastronomy master's degree candidate at Boston University, Carlos Olaechea, "What makes it [Tap Tap Restaurant] unique not only in Miami, but also in the United States, is that it is one of the few, if not only, Haitian restaurants that caters to non-Haitians by introducing the culture and cuisine. It is usually many non-Haitians' first taste of Haitian cuisine . . . that is, of course, unless they live in North Miami, North Miami Beach or close to Little Haiti [where the majority of the Haitian community in Miami resides]. It is considered a restaurant for *blan yo* [white people]. The fact that it is located in a relatively safe and touristy part of Miami Beach makes it accessible, not only physically but also socially and mentally, to outsiders wanting to experience Haitian culture."

Located in Miami Beach, Tap Tap does not follow the rapidly changing restaurant trends of its neighbors, but stays true to its original mission, which is to provide accessible Haitian food to the local community. Miami is home to one of the country's largest Haitian populations. Much like the rest of Miami's immigrants, the Haitian community came to create a better life and escape the brutal dictatorship of the Duvalier family, aka Papa Doc and Baby Doc. The majority of Haitians came to Miami in the eighties, but due to racial tensions, the community has not flourished as greatly as other ethnic groups.

Amidst the crazy era of the nineties, Tap Tap Restaurant emerged on a more quiet side of Miami Beach on Fifth Street. The restaurant's two-story white exterior is simple, cool, and collected and varies greatly from its interior with its flurry of colors and wall murals and every inch of space covered. Artist Joseph Wilfrid Daleus painted many of the murals on the walls, and when the art was created, Haiti was about to elect their first democratically elected leader. Different scenes from everyday Haitian life, from agriculture to religion and the arts, are portrayed. I especially like the images on the menus.

The name of the restaurant itself refers to the elaborately decorated public transportation found throughout Haiti, in which the bed of a pickup truck is outfitted with benches, and passengers tap the side of the vehicle to indicate their stop. A blue tap tap can be found outside the restaurant.

"The food seems to be secondary to the ambience, and it is the ambience that seems to attract people the most. Tap Tap is a starting point for people interested in Haitian cuisine. They use better ingredients than many of the other Haitian restaurants in Miami, including organic meats and Berkshire pork. They also feature certain dishes not commonly found at many Haitian restaurants like *chiktay*, a cod or herring salad." Haitian food is most closely related to soul food in the way the meats are marinated. Some of the restaurant's most popular dishes are *griot*, fried pork chunks with grilled onions and peppers; *poul boukanen*, grilled chicken with watercress sauce; *pwason gwo sèl*, whole snapper in lime sauce; and vegetable stew. Of course, there is no shortage of scotch bonnet, a staple of Haitian cuisine. Olaechea also notes that desserts like *pen patat*, a firm white yam pudding, and *blan manje*, a coconut custard, are popular, yet less known staples. The restaurant's house cocktail is called Soley and is made with aged rum [best with Rhum Barbancourt] and fresh passion fruit juice, and in a city where tropical drinks reign supreme; their mojito is touted as one of the best in Miami, using only the highest-quality fresh ingredients. Local rum expert Robert Burr gives Rhum Barbancourt five stars and is a personal favorite.

"Because it is owned by non-Haitians, the restaurant focuses on what is really unique about Haitian culture and does not try to appear European or Western. A lot of other Haitian restaurants such as Chez le Bebe and Chez Madame John, while being authentic in the food they serve, tend to minimize the African aspects of Haitian culture by conforming to Western standards of decor and even adopting French, rather than Creole, names for their restaurants that give the businesses an air of continental sophistication." Many other voodoo customs and holidays are observed offering a good platform for those wanting to learn more about the culture. Most interesting is the lead musician of the restaurant's resident band that performs at least twice a week. Manno Charlemagne served as mayor of Port-au-Prince between 1995 and 1999. In a city like Miami you never know what important individual you may be seated next to.

"It has always seemed to me that the purpose of Tap Tap is not so much to serve Creole cuisine as it is to provide a Haitian cultural experience that feels authentic and other, different from American culture and also from the many other Latin American and Caribbean cultures found in Miami. The restaurant almost functions like a dinner theater, where the dinner is secondary to the theater. The theater in the case of Tap Tap is the ambience, the live performances, and the dose of voodoo ephemera."

TITANIC RESTAURANT & BREWERY

5813 PONCE DE LEON BLVD. • CORAL GABLES, FL 33146

(305) 668-1742 • TITANICBREWERY.COM

Pint of Miami Beer History

In April 2014 Titanic Brewing Company celebrated their quinceañera, an important rite of passage for the heavily Hispanic community of Miami, and while fifteen years may not be a long period of time by normal standards, in Miami, it is a lifetime.

These days the beer scene is much more prominent, but for the better part of Miami's existence, it has been all about the umbrella-adorned cocktails. While the Abbey Brewing Company is older by four years, the location does not boast as much character as Titanic Brewery after it underwent a major renovation that removed a lot of its *je ne sais quoi*. Other than a brief blip on the beer radar with Regal Brewing Company in the thirties, Miami's beer scene did not exist prior to the opening of these two catalysts, the Abbey and Titanic.

"Titanic Brewery and the Abbey Brewing Company inspired me," says Diego Ganoza, owner of Gravity Brewlab. "Back in the nineties, the fact that someone could make their own beer was still a new and novel idea for me. Although they are competitors, they are both pioneers of the movement. They really just opened up my eyes to the possibilities. The idea for Gravity Brewlab began as a brewpub like Titanic, but ultimately, the restricting laws made it too difficult to come to fruition. I really give them so much credit.

"In Latin America, where most of Miami's population is from, it is most common to drink Heineken and Corona, because those were the only 'international' beers that were available in their countries. Most of us came with that tradition to the United States, and that is why

you see it so prevalent in restaurants around the city. It would take a movement and big pushing to change the traditions. Beer bars like Abraxas in Miami Beach and Cervezas in South Miami were influential in growing the scene in 2006. These beer bars worked hard with distributors to bring in new brews.

"The beer scene was truly solidified in 2010 and now it is a whole new world, with microbreweries popping up left and right. This second generation of brewers is similar to the food pioneers, in the late nineties and early 2000s when you saw chefs like Michelle Bernstein and Michael Schwartz, who worked under the Mango Gang, go out on their own. Young people who cut their teeth at iconic establishments like Titanic and the Abbey are at the helm of this second generation, pushing boundaries and yearning to infuse the local flavors of Miami, which is much different than the traditional styles found at the aforementioned establishments. This is why rare brews like guava sours and mango IPAs are so popular."

Internal rumblings of a beer scene began with the purchase of Tobacco Road by Kevin Rusk and Patrick Gleber in the eighties. Rusk would go on to open Titanic in 1999, long before the current burgeoning beer scene, which sprang up a little more than two years ago. Now everyone is buzzing about beer. Rusk had been running Tobacco

Road for twenty-plus years. The beer they served there was simply purchased; no real thought was put into it. In 1996 he decided to part ways with the equally iconic bar (he still maintains equity in the company) and study all aspects of the beer business.

"I spent time in the Northeast in about thirty different brewpubs," Rusk says. "Brewpubs were extremely popular in the late nineties. I also joined the Institute for Brewing Studies." While in the Northeast, he became fast friends with the guys from Shipyard Brewery and became a brewer's apprentice for them. "You have to be at the brewery to get unpasteurized fresh beer. I do not think many people know that little fact. I just love the science behind it all."

At Titanic, signature drafts include Triple Screw Light Ale, Captain Smith's Rye Ale, White Star India Pale Ale, Britannic Best Bitter, Boiler Room Nut Brown Ale, and Shipbuilders Oatmeal Stout. "Captain Smith's Rye Ale is my personal favorite; it is a German-style amber ale brewed with German pilsner and malted rye, producing a complex beer that is malty, fruity, and spicy. It finishes light and clean. It even won an award, one of the only breweries to win the Beer World Cup Award," says Rusk. On Untapped, a popular social beer app, Paul R. also comments on the beer: "Reliable. Satisfying. Fragile, Venetian lacing. Deep amber. Tasty." Titanic keeps it traditional with their brewing. In terms of the food, it is a straight-up pub fare, offering such classics as sausage and cheese, wings, fresh dolphin, and burgers. They map out the menu by beer pairing.

Vintage Spot
THE ABBEY BREWING COMPANY: EST. 1995

The Abbey is Miami's oldest brewpub and the city's beer forefather. They brew the traditional styles of beer: Immaculate IPA, Father Theodore's Stout, Brother Dan's Double, and Brother Aaron's Quadruple. Their wooden interior is reminiscent of European beer halls and monasteries, no passport required.

1115 16th St.; (305) 538-8110; abbeybrewinginc.com

Rusk initially wanted to open in Coconut Grove. He specifically had his eye on an original Masonic Temple on Main Highway. He eventually found the Coral Gables spot and opened on April 1, 1999. As for the highly recognizable name, they wanted to have one with an edge. "When we first opened Tobacco Road," Rusk explains, "everyone told us that we should change the name, as it had a negative connotation. We kept it because we liked the edge. Keith Wyness, a partner in a cruise line, suggested the name for Titanic. He said that if we tied the brewery to the cruise line industry, he could provide a steady stream of cruise members to the brewpub. This question always comes up. We named the brewpub before the movie *Titanic* came out."

TOBACCO ROAD

626 S. MIAMI AVE. • MIAMI, FL 33130

(305) 374-1198 • TOBACCO-ROAD.COM

Liquor License #1

*T*obacco Road is the everyman's (and woman's) bar. Opened in 1912, the popular two-story dive bar is usually featured at the top of everyone's must-try list when visiting Miami.

The Road, as it is most commonly referred to, is located in the heart of Brickell and surrounded by pricey high-rises and chic restaurants. But, it was not always like this. Before the area's construction boom in the early 2000s, the Road stood alone as a beacon in the night.

Over the course of its long history, it has operated as a Prohibition-era speakeasy, a gambling hall, a jazz club, a burlesque house, and a gay bar under the names the Chicken Roost, the Chanticleer Restaurant, and the Saiclere, to name just a few. In 1912 it fronted as a bakery appropriately called The Bakery, hiding a secret liquor room on its second floor. While Prohibition did not begin until 1920, the city battled with its own alcohol consumption as the temperance movement stormed through the city. The bootlegging business operated at an all-time high during this period, and The Bakery stood in the perfect location with easy access to the Miami River.

Patrick Gleber, its current owner, purchased the bar at the age of twenty-two from Michael Latterneralong, along with Kevin Rusk, who later went on to open Titanic Brewery in Coral Gables. Gleber is a Miami native and attended Florida International University's School of Hospitality. While all his friends left Miami, he decided to stay and make an impact. His inspiration was further sparked by an episode of *60 Minutes* on downtown gentrification. But opening a bar in Brickell

in 1982 was no easy feat. The establishment already donned the name Tobacco Road, but it was a gritty and rough dollar-beer and dollar-shot bar that had even earned the distinction of being one of the city's worst bars.

Initially, they only made around $150 a night, $300 to $400 if they were lucky. "In the first six months, I saw a guy get stabbed and another guy get shot in the stomach," says Gleber. "I would go into work with brass knuckles in my back pocket. This was a rough time all over Miami; the Marielitos were placed in temporary housing in a makeshift tent facility under the nearby highway overpass, and the Miami Vice era of drugs and violence was in full effect. Nobody wanted to come to downtown, much less a dive bar. I had never even gone into Tobacco Road before I purchased the place."

The day he went to see the property, four signs convinced him to pull the trigger: "Kevin and I visited Tobacco Road on St. Patrick's Day, a drinker's favorite holiday; the name Dee was written out in the cement in front of the bar's entrance, and that is my mom's nickname; there was a rabbit's foot in the gutter when we walked out; and the last sign which sealed the deal, the Nashville Teens' hit song 'Tobacco Road' played on the radio during my drive home. We did not have cell phones back then, so I could not call him on the spot. It was about 3 a.m. when I got home. I called him and the rest, as they say, is history."

Rich Ulloa, original owner of Yesterday and Today Records, which is also featured in this book, was once quoted as saying, "The place is iconic, a great gathering place for music and socializing." And it's true, Tobacco Road not only doled out cheap drinks, but also boosted interest in the local music scene, one of the first and still one of the only few that hosts live music shows in the city.

Patrick Gleber shares his favorite memory from years past: "In the early days at the Road, I gambled with my money bringing in blues shows for the second floor, a concept that was not popular at the time. I was bringing in amazing people such as Albert King, Barbara Dane, and Koko Taylor, the Queen of the Blues from Chicago. One night, Taylor was singing upstairs when the power went out. The professional that she is, she said, 'Does anyone have an acoustic guitar?' Someone from the audience went to grab one from their car and she continued singing in the dark for another hour, hour and a half. You lie awake and think of that, and you know you did something right with your life." The second-floor music lounge was eventually turned into an unused space.

In early 2014 the Cocktail Collection opened on the second floor. You could say it is a bar within a bar, as the vibe is completely different up there. Why now? Patrick just got tired of looking at the empty and dilapidating space, and simply, it was the natural next progression. Teaming up with Leo Holtzman, a Miami-based mixologist, they are revitalizing the speakeasy that first called the space home.

The Road is the Road is the Road. At the end of the day, the owners want one thing—for Tobacco Road to continue being the neighborhood spot for good drinks, good food, good music, and a good time. They are not trying to be ahead of the curve on anything. And one thing is always constant: Everyone knows that the Road is open until 5 a.m.; you can always stop there on your way home for a solid experience and a nightcap.

At printing time, a real estate developer purchased Tobacco Road's location to make way for a new high-rise development. Locals are working hard to have the government bestow the bar with historic designation. If not finalized in time, a rescue attempt will be salvaging any and every scrap of 626 S. Miami Ave. for use at 69 SW Seventh St., the tentatively proposed new location. This would mark the first move for the iconic establishment in 101 years.

VENETIAN POOL

2701 DE SOTO BLVD. • CORAL GABLES, FL 33134

(305) 460-5306 • THEVENETIANPOOL.COM

Dip into History

*I*n a city where the temperature rarely drops below 70 degrees Fahrenheit, pools are a standard luxury. Coral Gables' public swimming pool, the Venetian Pool, splashes all others out of the water. The pool is even listed on the National Register of Historic Places. The only other pool in the city that garners as much attention is the iconic private pool at the Raleigh Hotel for its interesting shape.

Following the land boom of the 1920s, George Merrick came to Miami to create Coral Gables, the Mediterranean city of his dreams. An opening ad for the historic pool in a 1924 newspaper stated: "The Venetian Casino has been in course of construction for more than a year, and is the foremost example of Coral Gables ideal of rendering practical needs in terms of harmonious beauty." Indeed, the pool is the best example of Merrick's master city plans and design ideals, featuring elaborate bridges, open corridors, porticos, palm trees, and even grottos, all reminiscent of Venice, Italy, hence the name Venetian Pool.

Designed by famous architect Phineas Paist, the 820,000-gallon pool is fed with springwater from an underground aquifer and drained and filled daily. Before the coral rock quarry was used as the base for the pool, it stood as a high mound near the city's outskirts. Limestone from the quarry was used to build the community's homes, leaving a giant hole that needed to be covered or filled. The area's surrounding homes continue the design motifs of the pool.

The pool opened as the Venetian Casino in 1924 with an elaborate Floral Fashion Review that included water sports. In those days the term "casino" alluded to fine summerhouses, public houses, or

buildings located in gardens or parks where one would sit, not gambling houses. The early days of the Venetian Pool were a hit, attracting the likes of Johnnie Weissmuller, Arne Borg, and, it is rumored,
Esther Williams.

Coral Gables' summerhouse hosted a variety of activities, from
swimming and diving exhibitions to beauty pageants, teas, and lun-
cheons to keep residents interested and to keep up with its most
direct competitor, the nearby Coral Gables Golf and Country Club.
The Venetian was best known for its grand orchestral concerts that
took place inside of the drained pool. Touted for its acoustics, Thursday nights took center stage as orchestra night and became a regular see-and-be-seen event with music by Jan Garber and his Coral
Gables Orchestra. To ensure downtowners were part of the mix, free
buses transported residents from downtown Miami and back.

These early events really pushed the boundaries of creativity and interest and set the tone for years to come. In 1925 William Jennings Bryan, Miami's first citizen, gave a series of lectures on Florida and its opportunities for investment. That same year, in December, an elaborate beauty pageant was held over seven days. Masterminded by George Merrick himself, he noted that the beauty of the pool could not be idealized until such an event was conceived. A Night of Enchantment featured water nymphs, live music, and shimmering lights.

After the collapse of the boom and the Hurricane of 1926, Merrick sold the pool to the city for $12,600. Valued at a much higher price in current times, the city has done an excellent job preserving its history and ensuring its continuity for many decades to come. Since 1959 it has also been the home of the Venetian Aquatic Club, which teaches children and adults Red Cross swimming.

The pool ranges from 4 to 8 feet deep, along with a 2-foot kiddy pool. With admission ranging from $4 to $8 in the low season and $6 to $12 in the high season, it is a popular destination for families, adventurers, and locals alike. The palatial pool is so big that even on crowded days, it does not feel overwhelming. In the wintertime, there are even fewer people paddling about.

In a *Miami Herald* article from August 17, 2000, a local resident, Jane Schmitt, spoke to the pool's significance and longevity: "It's one of those places that has generations of people with similar stories." Stories of a child's first successful swim, a first kiss inside one of the grottos, carefree summer days, nostalgia, and birthday celebrations. And while the pool no longer gets dolled up for the orchestra, it continues to provide a beautiful and romantic backdrop to life in "The City Beautiful."

WALL'S OLD FASHIONED ICE CREAM

8075 SW 67TH AVE. • MIAMI, FL 33143

(305) 740-9830 • WALLSICECREAM.COM

Life's Short, Eat Dessert First!

*D*id you know that the origins of ice cream could be traced back to the 4th century B.C.? The Roman Emperor Nero ordered ice to be brought from the mountains and combined with fruits, honey, and juices. It was known as "Sweet Ice." How about that the first real evidence of the existence of a form of "ice cream" originated in China's Tang period (AD 618–97)? King Tang of Shang had among his staff 94 "ice men" who helped to make a dish based on buffalo milk, flour, and camphor. Or finally, that the first ice cream parlor in America opened in New York City in 1776? All that and more can be found on the walls of Wall's Old Fashioned Ice Cream.

Because of its year-round balmy weather, ice cream is a full-time job in Miami. At Wall's, guests are provided a shot of groovy fifties nostalgia along with their frozen treats. It may not be the oldest ice cream shop around, but everything from their twenty-eight ice cream flavors to their decor and amenities are as vintage as it gets. The space, located directly across from another local institution, the Big Cheese, is often missed as it is small and hidden beneath lush palm trees. Look for the gravel parking lot and the outdoor stone tables covered by red and white sun umbrellas. Speaking of tiny, all kiddies under 36 inches receive a free baby cone. For your other babies, they give dogs a free doggie vanilla ice cream with your order. Most popular ice cream flavors include cookies 'n' cream, super hero, and raspberry sorbet. If you are not in the mood for ice cream, fret not; there is a rotating selection of twelve homemade fudge varieties,

smoothies, shakes, floats, and the Great Wall of Ice Cream, which consists of twelve scoops of ice cream, two wet toppings, two dry toppings, bananas, brownies, whipped cream, and a cherry on top. About that fudge, it is a one of a kind item in Miami; a secret I may have just spilled.

The store was originally founded by Jeff and Juliet Wall, hence the name. In 2005 it was taken over by Tom and Carol McKinney. Tom, a local Miamian with a background in the food business, beams with passion. In terms of Miami history, he is a wealth of information. On one such occasion when I visited, it was right after lunchtime and I had the place to myself for a good fifteen minutes. Just me, my cookie dough ice cream, and a mini trip to my childhood with old episodes of *Tom & Jerry*. Then, I was whisked on a historical journey of the establishment and "Miamah," as Tom pronounces it. Before moving across the street, the Big Cheese operated in Wall's tiny building. The interior floor of black and white tiles remains intact. What gets Tom most excited is the mini drive-in theater he created out front that shows old cartoons like *Mickey Mouse* and TV shows like *I Love Lucy* on a nightly basis, except for Saturday nights when a DJ spins the old fashioned tunes. It is a party on the gravel. History buffs will enjoy the artistic homage to Miami, which features drawings of old establishments like Holsum Bakery, the Orange Bowl and the old Parrot Jungle.

On any given day, you will find at least thirty kids hanging out and the line is usually a long one, at least eleven or twelve deep. The other main draw that sets this establishment apart from any other ice cream shop in town is that it truly is a haven for kids. There are not many places in town that cater to the specific demographic of children and teenagers, and the non-stop crowds show that they do it well. Be ready to become part of a community when you go. Visits to Wall's become shared experiences. Because the space is so small, it is normal for everyone to flow between each other's conversations. The other time I was there, someone at the front of the line ordered a smoothie. Soon everyone in the back wanted more details about this delicious looking concoction. By the time it got to my turn, four more folks had already ordered the drink. Adding to their generosity, the store promotes daily giveaways and participates in many events around town, mostly fund-raisers.

I leave you with one last ice cream fun fact. There are many stories about how the cone was born. There is a claim that Italo Marcioni patented the ice cream cone in 1903. Marcioni sold his homemade ice cream from a pushcart on Wall Street. He reduced his overhead caused by customers breaking or wandering off with his serving glasses by baking edible waffle cups with sloping sides and a flat bottom.

YESTERDAY AND TODAY RECORDS

9274 SW 40TH ST. • MIAMI, FL 33165

(305) 554-1020 • VINTAGERECORDS.COM

Analog in the Digital Age

Evan Chern's passion for music is what keeps Yesterday and Today Records, commonly referred to as Y&T, alive and grooving to the beats of the fifties, sixties, seventies, and eighties on Bird Road in Miami's suburbs, despite the economic climate that is making it difficult to operate such an establishment. "Even with the advent of great technology, vinyl will always be better, more natural, and warmer than digital music," says Chern.

The store is no larger than 1,000 square feet and houses approximately 50,000 records, using up every inch of space. Across the center aisle, unsorted vinyl tower over 6 feet and greet you the second you walk into the store. Fifty thousand records are only the tip of the musical iceberg: Chern's home garage overflows with twice the amount of records, but alas, there is just no space for it at the store. Elsewhere, you will find more bins with appropriately labeled music by genre; the records are in near-perfect condition, packed in sleeves that include a short paragraph detailing the history of the artist and their music. The store also sells CDs, cassettes, and 8-tracks, as well as the occasional T-shirt, poster, and memorabilia.

While the scene described above is the norm in record stores across the United States, such specialty stores are a rare find in Miami. In the past decade alone, Miami has seen the shuttering of popular shops like Blue Note Records in North Miami and even the downsizing of Y&T itself, having operated a total of three stores simultaneously at its peak—Yesterday Records for vintage finds, Today

Records for contemporary finds, and Y&T Dance servicing the DJ and dance music crowd. Even the popular South Florida–based corporate retailer Spec's Music shuttered the last of its stores in 2013. Miami is down to a handful of record stores, and Y&T is one of the oldest, having opened in June of 1981.

The store specializes in the fifties, sixties, seventies, and eighties, but Chern will occasionally stock newer records from artists like the Black Keys and Real Estate due to their mainstream popularity and high demand. A regular day at the store includes customers seeking new-release mainstream vinyl and EDM-style tracks, a specialty for DJs. Chern usually refers these customers to Sweat Records, another local record shop, which specializes in the more modern items.

Even if you're not into vinyl, a trip to the store is still worth the drive, as it sits like a music museum from another era. The store caters to the rare, old, eccentric, and hard to find. You are most likely to find the genres of jazz, blues, funk, soul, rock, garage, psychedelic, progressive, R&B, punk, alternative, disco, and Latino, but this is not an all-inclusive list. The general rule is no country, no opera, no classical music, no big band—anything else pretty much goes. "You never know what you may find, so you just have to come check it out for yourself. The collection is so large that I, myself, am sometimes surprised by the long-forgotten records I find," says Chern. Prices range from $1 to well over $500, but most are in the moderately priced $9.99 to $19.99 range.

Founded by another local, Rich Ulloa, Y&T has operated in different locations along the Bird Road corridor, where many of Miami's

Vintage Spot
FIFI'S RECORD SHOP: EST. 1980

Contrary to its name, the store does not sell vinyl. Located in the heart of Little Haiti, this unique store offers original Haitian music and movies in Creole. It is a catchall store that also sells items like flip-flops, hats, soft drinks, and soap.

159 NE 54th St., #1; (305) 756-5998

oldest establishments, such as Frankie's Pizza and Bird Bowl, still exist today. Since the early 2000s the store has been nestled on the second floor of a nondescript strip mall between a head shop and an Asian masseuse parlor, still on Bird Road. A Miami native, the mild-mannered Chern is a walking encyclopedia of music history, and the store is his museum collection. He officially took over ownership in 1997.

With roots in the community, the store participates in the local scene by donating vinyl to museums and special collections and actively supporting local musicians, especially those from the University of Miami music department. From time to time, movie and music video directors ask to use the retail space as a backdrop, and Chern always happily agrees. Chern is also the former host of the WDNA show *Notes from the Underground*, which ran for fifteen years.

Chern's favorite new pastime is educating the younger local community about vinyl. In recent years the store's demographic has changed dramatically. His clientele is younger. And while they are Internet savvy and tech friendly, they have a nostalgic yearning for the things they were not able to experience themselves. Most of the records sold at the store are sealed, but this is where the Internet works wonders. Any customer can come in and play a snippet of a song on their phone for free, and then decide whether or not to buy the vinyl. "I'll spill my knowledge to anyone that wants to hear it," says Chern.

In a *Miami Herald* article from January 8, 1995, titled "Yesterday and Today Records Prepares for Tomorrow," Ulloa spoke about the split of the stores into three distinct entities: "The key in the '90s, in any business is to specialize. We can't compete with the megastores. We wanted to position ourselves for the future." Maybe he knew what was coming, not in terms of splitting up the stores, but specialization.

As for Chern's favorite group, it is Jefferson Starship, formerly Jefferson Airplane, a psychedelic-turned-rock group from San Francisco. Hopefully, Chern will continue to build this city on vinyl and music knowledge.

Appendix A

FEATURED PLACES BY CATEGORY

Attractions
Cauley Square Historic Railroad
   Village, 37
Hialeah Park Racing &
   Casino, 83
Venetian Pool, 171

Bars
Churchill's Pub, 41
Fox's Sherron Inn, 76
Jazid, 90
Mac's Club Deuce, 108
Tobacco Road, 167

Barbecue Restaurant
Shorty's Bar-B-Q, 150

Bookstore
Fifteenth Street Books, 67

Bowling Alley
Bird Bowl, 30

Brewery
Titanic Restaurant &
   Brewery, 163

Cigar Factory/Store
El Titan de Bronze, 64

Clothing Stores
La Epoca, 101
Maya Hatcha, 114
Miami Twice, 118

Comic Book Store
A&M Comics, 1

Cuban Restaurants
El Rey de las Fritas, 61
Molina's Ranch Restaurant, 121

Delicatessen
Mainzer's German Deli, 111

Diners
Donut Gallery Diner, 57
S&S Diner, 139
Stephen's Restaurant, 153

**Food Markets / Specialty
   Food Stores**
Laurenzo's Italian Market, 105

Appendix B

FEATURED PLACES BY NEIGHBORHOOD

Appendix C

FEATURED PLACES BY YEAR OF ORIGIN*

1903: Cauley Square Historic Railroad Village, 37

1912: Tobacco Road, 167

1913: Joe's Stone Crab, 93

1915: Seybold Jewelry Building, 145

1924: Venetian Pool, 171

1925: The Clay Hotel, 45

1925: Hialeah Park Racing & Casino, 83

1926: The Biltmore Hotel, 26

1926: Mac's Club Deuce, 108

1930s: The Forge Restaurant, 73

1935: Colony Theatre, 49

1938: Royal Castle, 136

1938: S&S Diner, 139

1940: The Raleigh Hotel, 132

1945: Austin Burke, 18

1946: Fox's Sherron Inn, 76

1946: Jackson Soul Food, 87

1948: Pinecrest Wayside Market, 128

1951: Shorty's Bar-B-Q, 150

1954: Allen's Drug Store, 11

1954: Laurenzo's Italian Market, 105

1954: Stephen's Restaurant, 153

1954: Sunset Corners Fine Wine and Spirits, 156

1955: Frankie's Pizza, 80

1956: Bird Bowl, 30

1960s: Monty's Raw Bar, 125

1961: Sedano's Supermarket, 142

1962: Arbetter's Hot Dogs, 14

1965: La Epoca, 101

1967: Coopertown Restaurant, 53

1968: Maya Hatcha, 114

1970s: El Rey de las Fritas, 61

1971: Captain's Tavern Restaurant & Seafood Market, 33

1972: Donut Gallery Diner, 57

1972: Mainzer's German Deli, 111

1973: Football Sandwich Shop, 70

1973: La Casa de los Trucos, 98

1974: A&M Comics, 1

1978: A.C.'s Icees, 6

1979: Churchill's Pub, 41

1980: Beehive Natural Foods, 23

1980s: Fifteenth Street Books, 67

1981: Yesterday and Today Records, 177

1982: Molina's Ranch Restaurant, 121

1985: Miami Twice, 118

1994: Tap Tap Restaurant, 160

1995: El Titan de Bronze, 64

1996: Jazid, 90

1999: Titanic Restaurant & Brewery, 163

2002: Wall's Old Fashioned Ice Cream, 174

*Some years are approximate.

Photo Credits

All photographs by the author except the following:

Page v: Miami Beach; Courtesy of Phillip Pessar
Page xi: vintage car; Courtesy of Phillip Pessar
Page xv: Deauville Hotel; Courtesy of Phillip Pessar
Pages 3–4: A&M Comics; Courtesy of A&M Comics
Pages 8–9: A.C.'s Icees; Courtesy of Sef Gonzalez, Burger Beast
Page 12: Allen's Drug Store; Courtesy of Phillip Pessar
Page 15: Arbetter's Hot Dogs; Courtesy of Sef Gonzalez, Burger Beast
Page 27: The Biltmore Hotel; Courtesy of Phillip Pessar
Pages 46, 47: The Clay Hotel; Courtesy of The Clay Hotel
Pages 50, 52: Colony Theatre; Courtesy of Phillip Pessar
Page 62: El Rey de las Fritas; Courtesy of Javier Ramirez
Page 74: The Forge Restaurant; Courtesy of The Forge
Pages 77, 78: Fox's Sherron Inn; Courtesy of Fox's Sherron Inn
Page 84: Hialeah Park Race Track, 1991; Courtesy of Argelio Hernandez, photographer; HistoryMiami, 2005-531-2083
Page 88: Jackson Soul Food; Courtesy of Phillip Pessar
Page 94: Joe's Stone Crab (Joe's Stone Crab 1); Courtesy of Phillip Pessar
Page 96: Dinner at Joe's Stone Crab Restaurant, 1980; Courtesy of A. G. Montanari, photographer; Miami News Collection, History Miami, 1989-011-9155
Page 99: La Casa de los Trucos; Courtesy of Phillip Pessar
Page 103: La Epoca; Courtesy of La Epoca
Page 109: Mac's Club Deuce; Courtesy of Phillip Pessar
Page 119: Miami Twice; Courtesy of Colleen Merchant
Page 122: Molina's Ranch; Courtesy of Javier Ramirez
Page 133: The Raleigh Hotel pool, circa 1955; Courtesy of HistoryMiami, x-2045-1

Page 137: Royal Castle; Courtesy of Phillip Pessar
Page 140: S&S Diner; Courtesy of Phillip Pessar
Page 143: Sedano's Supermarket; Courtesy of Javier Ramirez
Pages 145, 146, 148: Seybold Jewelry Building; Courtesy of Phillip
   Pessar
Page 151: Shorty's Bar-B-Q; Courtesy of Phillip Pessar
Page 154: Stephen's Restaurant; Courtesy of Javier Ramirez
Page 161: Tap Tap Restaurant; Courtesy of HistoryMiami
Page 168: Tobacco Road; Courtesy of Marc Averette
Page 172: Venetian Pool, circa 1989; Courtesy of HistoryMiami, 2005-
   531-1675

Index

$16.95

8/12/15